RAY'S BOATHOUSE
Seafood Secrets of the Pacific Northwest

Text
KEN GOULDTHORPE

Food Photography
ANGIE NORWOOD BROWNE

Recipes
EXECUTIVE CHEF CHARLES RAMSEYER AND STAFF

Documentary Media LLC
Seattle, Washington

Ray's Boathouse: Seafood Secrets of the Pacific Northwest
Copyright © 2003 Documentary Media and Ray's Boathouse

First edition 2003
Second printing, 2006
Printed in Canada

Author: Ken Gouldthorpe
Recipes: Executive Chef Charles Ramseyer and Ray's Boathouse staff
Recipe Testing: Ray's Boathouse management and staff
Managing Editor: Petyr Beck
Food Photographer: Angie Norwood Browne
Food Stylist: Patty Wittmann
Contributing Photographer: Jaimie Trueblood
Copy Editor: Judy Gouldthorpe
Ray's Copy Editor: Lori Magaro
Designer: Nancy Gellos
Publisher: Barry Provorse

Library of Congress Cataloging-in-Publication Data

Gouldthorpe, Ken. 1928—
Ray's Boathouse: Seafood Secrets of the Pacific Northwest / text, Ken Gouldthorpe;
food photography, Angie Norwood Browne;
recipe development, Executive Chef Charles Ramseyer and Ray's Boathouse staff.
p. cm.
ISBN 0-9719084-2-7
1. Cookery (Seafood) 2. Cookery, American—Pacific Northwest style.
3. Ray's Boathouse (Restaurant)
I. Ramseyer, Charles. II. Ray's Boathouse (Restaurant) III. Title.
TX747.G68 2003
641.6'92—dc21   2003000161

Documentary Media LLC
3250 41st Avenue SW
Seattle, Washington 98116
(206) 935-9292
email: books@docmedia.org
www.documentarymedia.com

TABLE OF CONTENTS

9   The Essence of Ray's

25   The Art of Appetizers

49   Fresh Salads and Soups

67   Pacific Northwest Shellfish

81   Cold-Water Crustaceans

95   Wild Salmon

115   White Fish

139   Perfect Endings

165   Northwest Wine Cellar

166   Guide to Special Ingredients

170   Acknowledgments

172   Index

THE ESSENCE OF RAY'S

Not So Much a Fish House as a Phenomenon

TWO DAYS AFTER I FIRST CAME TO SEATTLE FROM MANHATTAN SOME 24 YEARS AGO, A BALLARD NATIVE TOOK ME TO RAY'S CAFE FOR LUNCH. IT WAS ONE OF THOSE GLORIOUS AFTERNOONS ("RAY'S DAYS," AS THE LOCALS CALL THEM) JUST MADE FOR sitting out on an open deck overlooking what must be one of the grandest views in God's creation. To be honest, my expectations weren't too high, as I'd been warned by certain New Yorkers that "there wasn't much worth eating out there north of San Francisco." But the grilled wild king salmon presented to me on that memorable day was, to say the least, a total surprise—no, make that revelation. Soft, moist and utterly impeccable, it had a unique delicate texture that led me to scorn its farm-raised Atlantic cousin forever.

Come to Ray's at around 7 o'clock on a warm summer evening. In the classic Boathouse Restaurant, sitting just a few feet above the Puget Sound waterline at high tide, guests settling into their private booths or seated at window tables scan the wide reaches of the Sound and the soaring Olympic Mountains beyond from the comfort of their surroundings, watching the maritime traffic heading to and from the Hiram Chittenden Locks. Here crisply attired servers present the evening's specials and suggest entrées from the inviting menu and appropriate wines from Ray's award-winning cellar. It is solid, snug and intimate here, polished yet neither prim

Sunny days, tall ships, or just about any other excuse fills the deck at Ray's.

nor prudish, a place to enjoy with old friends and family even when the rain falls or the snow flies, a place to remember vows that were made, to celebrate anniversaries, or just to contemplate good things to come.

Upstairs in the bustling Cafe, people are crowding the landing, hoping for space to open up on the deck or in the bar, already a hive of activity. Attractive young singles, families with tots, silver-haired seniors and college kids with dates—they're all here. The Cafe servers, comfortable in shorts and tees, waltz from table to table, answering questions, offering suggestions, advising the undecided. Bussers swiftly remove dishes and refill water glasses, food runners deftly tote trays through this wonderfully controlled chaos, while out on the deck, diners basking in the brilliant sunshine gossip and nibble as they look out at a view that never fails to thrill locals and visitors alike. The staff serves a full house of guests with the calculated ease and efficiency that makes them exceptional at their craft.

As the evening wears on, a slight breeze cools the deck, and blankets are broken out for those who request them. The sky by now is a glowing multicolored panorama that would do justice to a Turner painting, and at sunset, when diners elsewhere are sequestered inside, those here are bathed in a golden afterglow that only the cosmos can bestow. Later, relaxed and at ease, they sit sipping after-dinner drinks in the gathering dusk. By midnight, some are still here, swathed in

blankets and loath to leave. Down in the Boathouse Restaurant, guests linger over an array of house-made desserts, vintage ports and succulent local cheeses. Next door, Ray's has catered a wedding party in its beautifully set private banquet room, and the celebration continues over the last of the cake and champagne by moonlight. This is the Ray's experience—the Boathouse at its best.

Words like *iconic* and *quintessential* have all too frequently been used to describe this singular restaurant, but it's hard to find more appropriate adjectives. Tucked away in a secluded Seattle neighborhood, it ranks among the world's exceptional seafood houses. While its product certainly ensures its lodgment among the best, its reputation was built not necessarily on haute cuisine, but rather on its total commitment to superior seafood native to the Pacific Northwest, and to a progressive learning curve that continues inexorably upward. Significantly, Ray's long ago transformed the conventional treatment of salmon hereabouts from something routinely baked, poached or casually cooked on a grill—and largely overdone—into an entrée so subtle and savory that neither fire nor flood could keep the crowds away.

In the early 1950s, excited kids and parents crowd the dock for the annual Kids' Dock-Fishing Derby at Ray's Boathouse.

In the beginning, a trio of investors—whose knowledge of seafood was pretty much limited to sports fishing—decided to take over the location of Ray Lichtenberger's famed old boathouse and café on Shilshole Bay and transform it into a quality restaurant. They were led by the indefatigable Russ Wohlers, a self-described "good ol' farm boy" from east of the Cascades who is in fact a gifted, multi-talented maverick driven by the pursuit of perfection. The would-be owners sensed that in this paramount location, the skillful presentation of the region's phenomenal seafood could turn the modest old café and rental-boat site into, yes, a Seattle icon, no easy task when you consider that the Seattle of thirty years ago, though blessed with a statewide spectrum of superlative fixings, was hardly a gourmet's paradise.

What the partners lacked in restaurant ownership experience they more than made up for with unbridled energy and enthusiasm. "It was a young, smart, swashbuckling, hands-on, walking-the-floors owner-manager group up for trying new things," recalls one-time fisherman and Seattle seafood guru Jon Rowley, one of Ray's early consultants. "They wanted to be the best, and they facilitated what it took to do it." That meant paying more for the product, developing—and rewarding—a loyal workforce imbued with the concept of excellence across the board, and attracting savvy chefs who understood or quickly learned about the delicate nature of wild salmon and the subtleties of extraordinary shellfish at a time when the public palate was nowhere near as demanding as it is today. Thus began a fusion of seafood learning and teaching seeded by the reality of the restaurant's upscale requirements and a marketplace in which excellence had to be sought out.

While the product itself was an essential prerequisite, the formula had to include the right mix of people, too, and the need for management to educate the kitchen staff and servers was equally critical. The crew had to become emotionally involved with what was being offered to the diner. Rather than just parroting the specials of the day, servers were required to taste what was being offered at sampling sessions on a daily basis so that they could speak of the food with authority. They had to, and still have to, be aware of precisely what came out of the kitchen and, remarkably, were empowered to question anything they considered less than perfect and to take it back—sacrilege in many restaurants where the hierarchy brooks no nonsense from commoners.

"Being passionate about what you do is paramount at Ray's," confides Wayne Ludvigsen, a twenty-year veteran who rose from dishwasher to chef at Ray's. "It's not something you learn. The confidence and commitment have to be there to begin with." And when new concepts and techniques were added to a high degree of professionalism overall, breakthroughs that affected the whole community's attitude toward seafood were bound to happen. And happen they did.

In the 1980s, when Rowley and Ludvigsen were working with Mauny Kaseburg, a canny food specialist with perhaps the most fastidious palate in the city, Ray's really began to hit its stride. "It was a magical time," she remembers. "Seattle's culinary reputation was booming, and Ray's was setting new standards, doing things that were the envy of its competitors. We would bring up menu ideas predicated on Northwest seafood of every stripe to the near exclusion of all foreign fish, no matter how popular they were."

And, ah, the oysters! The philosophy in serving an array of these velvety local bivalves as an appetizer was as much economic as gastronomic, according to Rowley. "If you can master oysters," he reasoned, "then you will attract food buffs who understand that oysters are only the prelude to a great meal."

Other establishments didn't have the same objectives. They might have had the view, but they didn't have the attitude. There is, after all, a vast difference between the corporate mind-

set and the personal touch of individual partners who honestly believe that they share the responsibility for Ray's success equally with their employees, for whom the seeds of company fidelity were sown very early on. As partner Earl Lasher, who worked with Wohlers from the very beginning, recalls: "Back then we were about the same age as our crew and most of our guests, so we did the same things, played the same games, lived pretty much the same lives, and shared the same worries and triumphs. We were in sync, a team. Our guests got it, and so did the staff." They still do.

Ray's Boathouse owners (from left) Elizabeth Gingrich, Russ Wohlers, Earl Lasher and Jack Sikma

So do the owners. Elizabeth Gingrich, who came aboard in 1977, readily admits that in the beginning as a new partner, she needed to know much more about how a restaurant works. "So they had me do the books. I was terrible at it. Wasn't my thing. But it was a terrific part of my life. I never felt like an owner because the staff made me feel I was one of them." She shares with fellow partners Wohlers, Lasher and the newest team player, Jack Sikma, a rare blend of admiration, respect and pride of ownership spurred by their love of involvement. And as a pioneer in the betterment of the Northwest dining experience, Ray's has achieved a standard of excellence that has helped make it a household word.

Ray's Wine Director and staff sample the work of new vintners and vintages.

How did they do it? Well, the original philosophy was simple enough. They hired the best people they could find, and gave them a full measure of responsibility as professionals serving the public, building confidence as they went, along with expertise in the food and wines they presented. "It's been a long evolution," says Gingrich. "Today we're far more sophisticated than we were in our approach to the entire dining experience."

Ray's Boathouse Executive Chef Charles Ramseyer

The person who has been essentially driving that sophistication for the past decade is Executive Chef Charles Ramseyer, a classically trained Swiss native whose eclectic culinary career was honed in Zurich and in upscale kitchens around the globe. The basics of Ludvigsen's era—great seafood simply prepared—remain, but as Wayne himself puts it, "I was trained in Ballard, and I knew a lot about a little. Charles was trained in Europe, and what's in his impressive repertoire he learned in the kitchens of the world."

But Ramseyer admits he had much more to learn about fish when he came to Ray's.

In the European tradition, seafood is an appetizer or a side dish, he says, and the presentation is far from being focused on the fish itself. Ramseyer is essentially a *saucier*, complementing superb ingredients with exquisite toppings, salsas, chutneys and dressings. At Ray's, where seafood dominates, he had to relearn the whole process from buying the product to the nuances of its preparation. "Fish is such a sensitive product," he says. "King is rich, sockeye is delicate, sturgeon is mild, and you can really overpower it—and so you must learn how to bring out the specific flavor in each rather than to disguise it. My concentration has

been on the chutneys and local berry- and fruit-based creations that allow the fish to remain supreme."

In developing his significant and broad-based skills, Ramseyer credits—with no little incredulity—the attitude of management and partners at Ray's, who empowered him with the autonomy he needed to develop his own ideas and concepts. "This is not the case in many other establishments, where management tells you what they want and makes no bones about it. Here, they listen to me, and their flexibility in trying new things is exceptional, so we're creating things as a team. Every recipe in this book represents a team effort. This is why I'm so inspired. They let me take the restaurant to another level without destroying those things that made Ray's exceptional in the first place."

Executive Chef Charles Ramseyer at a preshift meeting

Ramseyer spots in-house talent and encourages it. One kitchen hand had a knack for smoking salmon, cod and scallops so perfectly that they are now part of a Ray's signature dish. And despite the fact that this is still a family restaurant without pretense—a local restaurant, insist the partners, "and always will be"—any guest in the main dining room cannot fail to be impressed by the food and the fastidious service. The consistent quality and innovation have made the Ray's dining experience famous, winning for Ray's the nationally acclaimed James Beard Foundation America's Classic Award in New York in 2002, and too many other commendations to mention. Sums up Ramseyer with the contented smile of a happy man: "Ray's is my passion. I may have learned in other restaurants, but this one I call my own."

And so it is that a small dockside café originally owned by a convivial Will Rogers look-alike has grown into the icon that the partners hoped for thirty years ago. In that time, most of Seattle's other long-established and beloved classic restaurants have disappeared. Ray's, however, has weathered a changing and fickle marketplace, survived a devastating fire that would have terminated most restaurants, but was seized upon by Ray's as an opportunity for new growth, and emerged even more cosmopolitan and cultivated than before. Its carefully balanced wine cellar has introduced many Pacific Northwest wines whose names are now esteemed by the nation's connoisseurs, and the experimentation with palatable pairings—those compositions with a common thread that gives the meal its edge—continues apace.

Elizabeth Gingrich perhaps best sums up the soul and the sensitivity of Ray's. "Ray's grew through a sense of love and dedication," she says, "but part of our growth was to let go, to hold it close with our arms wide open."

There is perhaps no better advice in the practical enjoyment of home cooking than to hold the recipes close—but to keep the mind wide open.

Bon appétit!

THE ART OF APPETIZERS

Savory Starters

APPETIZERS, A FORM OF GUSTATORY TITILLATION PAVING THE WAY FOR THE HEAVY-WEIGHT MAIN COURSE, ARE THE PERFECT ACCOMPANIMENT FOR A COCKTAIL OR AN EXCEPTIONAL WINE. THEY COME IN LITERALLY THOUSANDS OF GUISES, BUT AT RAY'S, appetizers are always down-to-earth and fun. They're a wonderful greeting between friends, or a getting-to-know-you preamble between strangers before they take on more serious conversation over more substantial platters. At Ray's, of course, the appetizers are totally seafood oriented, entirely wonderful. Here, the genius of the preparers comes into play, for today's appetizer can be so delectable—and substantial—that the light diner often prefers one or two of these elegant concoctions instead of a regular entrée.

Some are basic, straightforward, like crisped calamari. Others, like the savory Thai Mussels, are an imaginative combination of flavors. But at Ray's, they always embrace those local elements for which Washington has become famous—salmon and shellfish, smoked, steamed or poached or on the half shell, accompanied by exquisite seasoned broths, dipping sauces or chutneys made from the state's abundance of seasonal berries and fruit. "At all times," submits Chef Ramseyer, "we look for what works well with the flavor of the seafood—mango and shrimp have perfect balance, for example, or smoked scallops with fennel-horseradish cream." And for those who wish to indulge themselves in the whole nine fathoms, Ray's can—and does—put all of these items on one great sampler platter: smoked scallops, prawns, plump oysters, mussels and crab, a veritable taste of the Pacific Northwest for both visitors and those of us who don't need a passport.

Ray's Cafe Seafood Margarita

4 jumbo prawns, cooked and peeled (8-12 per pound)
4 ounces bay shrimp, cooked
2 ounces cooked Dungeness crabmeat
6 segments of lime
6 segments of orange
1/2 cup cubed mango
2 tablespoons chopped cilantro
2 teaspoons fresh lime juice
Kosher salt

GARNISH:
2 radicchio leaves
2 curly endive leaves
Crispy corn chips
Cilantro sprigs

Dice 2 of the jumbo prawns. Butterfly the remaining 2 prawns by cutting lengthwise down the backs. In a medium bowl, mix diced prawns, butterflied prawns, shrimp, crabmeat, lime segments, orange segments, mango, cilantro and lime juice. Season with salt to taste and marinate in refrigerator for 15 minutes. Line 2 chilled margarita glasses with radicchio and endive. Spoon mixture into glasses and garnish with corn chips and cilantro sprigs. Serve immediately.

SERVES 2.

Thai Mussels

1 cup coconut milk
2 teaspoons fresh lime juice
1 teaspoon red curry paste
2 teaspoons Thai fish sauce
2/3 cup sake
1 teaspoon minced garlic
1 teaspoon minced fresh ginger
1 teaspoon chopped fresh basil
2 pounds Penn Cove mussels,
   cleaned and debearded

GARNISH:
2-4 sprigs basil

In a large bowl, whisk
together coconut milk,
lime juice, curry paste,
fish sauce, sake, garlic,
ginger and basil.

Heat a heavy saucepan
over high heat for about
30 seconds. Add mussels
and broth. Bring to a boil
and reduce heat. Cover
and simmer for about
5 minutes, or until
mussels fully open.

Divide mussels into bowls
and serve with broth and
plenty of crusty bread.
SERVES 4.

**To ensure the safety and
quality of the shellfish, make
sure mussels are alive and shells
are closed. Always purchase
from a reputable fishmonger.**

Dungeness Crab & Corn Fritters
WITH SWEET CHILI DIPPING SAUCE

2-3 quarts canola oil for frying
1 cup all-purpose flour
1 1/2 teaspoons kosher salt
1/2 teaspoon ground white pepper
1/2 teaspoon granulated garlic
1/2 teaspoon cayenne pepper
1 1/2 teaspoons baking powder
1/4 cup milk
2 large eggs, beaten
1 1/2 teaspoons unsalted butter, melted
3/4 cup Dungeness crabmeat
1/2 cup frozen corn kernels
1/2 cup diced red bell pepper
1/2 cup diced green onion

Set up a deep fryer (see page 44) and heat oil to 350°F. Note: Monitor temperature carefully. If the oil is too hot, the outside of the fritters will burn before the inside has cooked.

In a mixing bowl, combine flour, salt, white pepper, granulated garlic, cayenne pepper and baking powder. In a separate bowl, combine milk, eggs, butter, crabmeat, corn, red bell pepper and green onion and mix well. Add to dry ingredients and mix with a fork until just combined. Do not overmix. Drop batter by heaping tablespoonfuls into hot oil. Cook until fritters are golden brown and fully cooked on the inside, about 3 to 5 minutes. Using a slotted spoon, transfer fritters to a plate lined with a paper towel to drain. Serve immediately, accompanied by dipping sauce.

YIELD: 18 FRITTERS; SERVES 4 TO 6.

Sweet Chili Dipping Sauce

1/4 cup freshly squeezed lemon juice
2 teaspoons minced garlic
1/4 cup light brown sugar
2 teaspoons sambal oelek
2 tablespoons water
2 tablespoons Thai fish sauce

In a small bowl, whisk together lemon juice, garlic, brown sugar, sambal oelek and water. Then add fish sauce and stir just until combined. YIELD: 2/3 CUP.

Grilled Salmon Skewers

WITH SPICED PEACH-CURRANT CHUTNEY

2 6-ounce salmon fillets, skin removed
12 6-inch wood or metal skewers
Olive oil
Kosher salt
Freshly ground black pepper

Prepare a charcoal or gas grill.

Cut salmon fillets into 12 pieces, about 3 inches long by 1/2 inch thick. Skewer salmon pieces lengthwise and brush generously with olive oil. Season both sides of salmon with salt and pepper to taste.

Grill salmon skewers over medium-high heat just until the center of each piece becomes opaque, about 1 to 2 minutes on each side. Serve immediately with Spiced Peach-Currant Chutney.

SERVES 4 TO 6.

Spiced Peach-Currant Chutney

1 tablespoon canola oil
1/2 cup diced white onion
5 tablespoons light brown sugar
1 teaspoon yellow mustard seed
1 teaspoon ground cumin
1/2 teaspoon curry powder
1 teaspoon cinnamon
1/2 teaspoon nutmeg
1/2 teaspoon ground allspice
Pinch ground cloves
1 teaspoon kosher salt
Pinch white pepper
4 cups sliced IQF (individually quick-frozen) peaches
5 tablespoons orange juice concentrate
1/2 cup white wine vinegar
5 tablespoons dried currants
1 tablespoon finely diced green bell pepper
1 tablespoon finely diced red bell pepper

In a large saucepan, heat oil over medium-high heat until it just begins to smoke. Add onion and sauté until translucent. Add brown sugar, mustard seed, cumin, curry powder, cinnamon, nutmeg, allspice, cloves, salt and pepper. Stir until well blended. Add peaches, orange juice concentrate and vinegar. Bring mixture just to a boil, then reduce heat to low and simmer for 20 minutes. Remove from heat and transfer mixture to a heat-safe bowl. Stir in currants and peppers. Place uncovered bowl in refrigerator to cool. Cover after completely cooled. YIELD: 1 PINT.

Coconut Prawns
WITH SESAME PLUM SAUCE

2-3 quarts canola oil for frying

SEASONED FLOUR:
3 tablespoons flour
1 teaspoon kosher salt

BATTER:
1/2 cup milk
1 cup flour
2 large eggs
2 teaspoons kosher salt
1/4 teaspoon curry powder

COATING:
2 cups unsweetened flaked coconut
2 cups panko bread crumbs

24 prawns (16-20 per pound), tail on

Set up a deep fryer (see page 44) and heat oil to 300°F.

Set up 3 bowls. In the first bowl, combine flour and salt. In the second bowl, combine milk, flour, eggs, salt and curry powder to make a batter. In the third bowl, combine flaked coconut and panko.

Holding the tail, dredge each prawn in the seasoned flour and gently shake off excess. Then, dip prawn in batter. Third, toss prawn in coconut mixture to coat completely and pat gently to press mixture into batter.

Deep-fry immediately until golden, about 30 seconds. Using a slotted spoon, transfer prawns to a plate lined with a paper towel to drain. Serve warm with Sesame Plum Sauce. SERVES 6.

Sesame Plum Sauce

1 cup plum sauce
2 tablespoons mirin
2 tablespoons rice wine vinegar
1 tablespoon toasted sesame oil
1 teaspoon sambal oelek
1 tablespoon dry sherry
Pinch powdered ginger
1/2 teaspoon black sesame seeds
1/2 teaspoon sesame seeds

Combine all ingredients and mix well.

Smoking at Home

TO CONSERVE FOOD YEAR-ROUND, NATIVES OF THE PACIFIC NORTHWEST USED SLOW-BURNING GREEN ALDER FOR SMOKING FISH, CLAMS, OYSTERS AND WILD GAME. ALTHOUGH ORIGINALLY USED FOR PRESERVING FOODS, SMOKE IS NO LONGER simply a means of curing and drying. Today, smoke is appreciated for the superlative flavor it adds to food, and years ago Ray's kitchen staff perfected the art of smoking. A refrigerator-sized smoke-chamber with oven-sized racks stands in the restaurant's kitchen, where Ray's chefs slow-cook freshly caught seafood.

There are many options for smoking foods at home, but the basics are simple enough. The object is to get the wood chips hot enough to smoke but not burn, and you don't need elaborate temperature-controlled smokers with automatic timers to do that. A standing kettle grill or gas grill will do the job perfectly—with just a dash of TLC.

2 CUPS FRUITWOOD OR ALDER CHIPS

1 DISPOSABLE FOIL PAN, A CAST IRON SKILLET OR A BASKET MADE FROM SEVERAL SHEETS OF ALUMINUM FOIL

GAS GRILL OR CHARCOAL GRILL

Soak the wood chips in water for 2 to 4 hours, as desired, drain and then place in the foil pan.

For a gas grill, place the foil pan on top of the lava rocks or metal grids of one of the gas burners. Turn the burner on high heat until the chips begin to smoke, then reduce the heat to low. Increase the heat as needed just so that the chips continue to smoke.

For a charcoal grill, pile the charcoal in the center of the grill and start as usual. Once the coals have reached maximum heat, spread them out in a flat layer and place the foil pan of wood chips on top of the coals.

Close the lid and heat until the smoke seeps out thickly. Place food on the top shelf of the grill and close the lid. Adjust the vents, or open the lid slightly, to control the temperature and amount of smoke, and cook according to your recipe.

Thai Hong, Ray's in-house smoking expert

Smoked Salmon Cubes

1/2 cup light brown sugar
1/4 cup kosher salt
2 tablespoons water
1 pound king or coho salmon, cut into 1-inch cubes

Combine brown sugar, salt and water to make
a brine. Add salmon cubes and toss to coat evenly.
Marinate salmon in the refrigerator for 30 minutes.
Remove salmon from the marinade and drain excess
brine but do not rinse. Air-dry or use a household
fan to dry the cubes, turning occasionally to ensure
even drying, until the flesh is firm and the surface
feels tacky, about 1 to 2 hours.

Prepare a smoker with applewood or alder chips.
Place salmon cubes on the top rack and hot-smoke
until they are a rich, caramelized brown and the
translucency has just left the center, about 20 to
25 minutes, depending on the temperature in your
smoker. SERVES 4.

Ray's Pink Scallops
IN WHITE WINE & ROASTED RED PEPPER

1 red bell pepper
4 tablespoons unsalted butter
2 teaspoons chopped garlic
1/4 cup chopped shallots
2 pounds pink scallops
1/2 cup Sauvignon Blanc
2 teaspoons chopped fresh parsley
1 teaspoon chopped fresh thyme

To roast the pepper, broil in the oven or char over the flame of a gas burner until the skin has blackened. Place in a paper or plastic bag and seal the bag. When the pepper is cool enough to touch, remove and cut it in half. Discard the seeds and white membrane. Wash the pepper under cold running water and peel off the blackened skin, pat dry and dice.

In a 3-quart saucepan, melt butter over medium heat and sauté garlic and shallots until translucent. Add the scallops, wine, roasted red pepper, parsley and thyme. Cover the pan and cook until scallops open, about 2 minutes. Serve immediately.

SERVES 4.

**Manila clams
arrived in
the Pacific
Northwest
from Japanese
waters in
the 1930s as
hitchhikers
among Pacific
oysters.**

Manila Clams
STEAMED IN WHITE WINE AND DILL BUTTER

3 pounds Manila clams
1/2 cup unsalted butter, softened
1 teaspoon dried dill weed
1 teaspoon kosher salt
1 cup Chardonnay

Rinse clams under cold running water to remove any sand from the shells. In a small bowl, mix together butter, dill and salt. In a 3-quart sauté pan over medium heat, combine clams, dill butter and wine. Cover pan and bring to a boil. Cook for about 5 to 6 minutes, shaking the pan or stirring occasionally, until all the shells open. Discard any clams that do not open. Serve immediately. SERVES 4.

Pacific Oysters on a Spoon

24 medium-sized fresh Pacific oysters in the shell,
    or 1 jar extra-small shucked Pacific oysters
1/2 cup Sauvignon Blanc
1/2 cup fish stock or water
1/2 cup heavy cream
Kosher salt
Freshly ground black pepper

24 Chinese ceramic soup spoons

GARNISH SUGGESTIONS:
2 tablespoons chopped chives or parsley
1 tablespoon tobiko caviar

Shuck the oysters, saving the oyster nectar, and place in a bowl. (Trim the abductor muscle with scissors, if desired.)

In a 2 1/2-quart saucepan, bring the wine and stock to a boil. Drop in the oysters and their nectar and poach until the oysters are plump and opaque, about 1 minute. Remove the oysters and place on warmed spoons. Keep warm. Over medium-high heat, reduce the remaining liquid by half. Add the cream and bring the mixture back to a boil. Reduce the mixture until thickened, about 5 minutes. Season sauce with salt and pepper to taste and spoon over the oysters. Garnish with chives, parsley or caviar. Serve immediately. SERVES 4 TO 6.

Smoked Scallops
WITH FENNEL-HORSERADISH CREAM

1/2 cup light brown sugar
1/4 cup kosher salt
1 pound sea scallops (10-20 per pound)

Combine brown sugar and salt in a medium bowl and mix well to make a dry brine. Add the scallops and toss to coat thoroughly. Marinate in the refrigerator for 45 minutes. Remove scallops from the brine (do not rinse) and spread on a rack. Air-dry or use a household fan to dry the scallops, turning occasionally to ensure even drying, until they are firm and the coating is tacky, about 1 to 4 hours, depending on the method of drying.

Prepare a smoker with applewood or alder chips (see page 32). Place scallops on the top rack and hot-smoke until they are a rich, caramelized brown and the translucency has just left the center, about 20 to 25 minutes, depending on the temperature in your smoker. Serve with Fennel-Horseradish Cream. SERVES 4.

Fennel-Horseradish Cream

1/2 fennel bulb (about 1/4 pound), top trimmed, finely diced
1/2 cup sour cream
1 1/2 tablespoons prepared horseradish
1 teaspoon fresh lemon juice
Kosher salt to taste
Ground white pepper to taste

Place fennel in a small saucepan and cover with water. Bring to a boil and continue boiling until the fennel is mushy, adding more water as needed. Drain the fennel and set aside to cool. When cool, squeeze the fennel to remove excess moisture. In a small bowl, mash fennel with a fork and then whisk in sour cream, horseradish, lemon juice, salt and pepper until well combined. This can be made a day in advance and refrigerated. YIELD: 1 CUP.

Shrimp Spring Rolls
WITH SWEET CHILI DIPPING SAUCE

8 sheets 12-inch round rice paper
4 leaves red-leaf lettuce
1 cup julienned napa cabbage
1 1/3 cups fresh bean sprouts
12 Thai mint leaves
4 green onions, green part only, cut in 6- to 8-inch sticks
1/2 bunch cilantro (2-3 sprigs per roll)
6 ounces cooked bay shrimp
2 cups rice noodles, cooked

Dip 1 sheet of rice paper in a bowl of lukewarm water and place on a plate or waxed paper. Dip a second sheet in water and layer on top of the first sheet. Allow rice paper to soften, about 1 to 3 minutes. Place a lettuce leaf on top of the softened rice paper. In the center of the lettuce leaf, layer 1/4 of the cabbage, bean sprouts, mint leaves, green onions, cilantro, shrimp and rice noodles. Wrap the sides of the lettuce leaf around the filling. Roll one side of the rice paper over the filling and pull gently toward you to pack the filling. Next, fold over the ends. Continue rolling to create a neat, tight package like an eggroll. Repeat with remaining rice paper. Slice spring rolls on a diagonal and serve with Sweet Chili Dipping Sauce (see page 29).

SERVES 4.

Pesto-Marinated Prawns

1/2 cup packed chopped fresh basil
1/4 cup pine nuts
1 tablespoon chopped garlic
1/2 cup olive oil
1/2 teaspoon kosher salt
Pinch black pepper
1 pound prawns (16-20 per pound), peeled, deveined, tail on
1 lemon, cut in half

In a blender, combine basil, pine nuts, garlic,
olive oil, salt and pepper. Blend until well combined,
scraping down sides of blender. This can be made
a day in advance and refrigerated.

In a bowl, combine prawns and basil marinade
and toss to coat evenly. Cover and marinate in the
refrigerator at least 4 hours or overnight.

Heat a grill or nonstick pan to medium-high. Remove
prawns from the marinade and place on the grill or in
the pan. Squeeze the lemon halves over the prawns and
cook until they are no longer translucent in the center,
about 1 minute on each side. Serve warm or chilled.

SERVES 4.

Shrimp-Stuffed Artichokes

4 artichokes
2 lemons, cut in half
Herbed Cream Cheese
8 ounces cooked bay shrimp

Slice half an inch off the top of each artichoke. Cut off the sharp tips of the leaves with scissors. Score an X on the bottom (stem side) of each artichoke. Rub all cut surfaces with one lemon half. Place the artichokes in a large pot and fill with water to cover. Squeeze the juice of the remaining three lemon halves into the water. Place a plate on top of the artichokes to keep them submerged. Bring the water to a boil, reduce heat and simmer until the outer leaves are tender and can be pulled off easily, about 30 to 40 minutes. Remove artichokes and turn upside down on a plate to cool, or refrigerate.

When the artichokes are cool, turn them upright and spread the inner leaves apart slightly. Scoop out the fuzzy chokes, leaving the heart intact. Remove a few of the center leaves to create a cup. Scoop Herbed Cream Cheese into artichokes. Top each artichoke with 2 ounces bay shrimp. Serve immediately.

SERVES 4.

HERBED CREAM CHEESE:
8-ounce package cream cheese, softened
3/4 cup mayonnaise
1/2 cup grated Parmesan cheese
1 tablespoon fresh lemon juice
1 teaspoon Worcestershire sauce
1 medium shallot, minced
1/4 cup minced celery leaves
1 teaspoon celery salt
2 teaspoons dried tarragon
1 teaspoon dried basil

In the bowl of an electric mixer, beat cream cheese until soft. Add mayonnaise, Parmesan, lemon juice, Worcestershire sauce, shallot, celery leaves, celery salt, tarragon and basil. Mix well.

Pesto-Marinated Sea Scallops

1/2 cup packed chopped fresh basil
1/4 cup pine nuts
1 tablespoon chopped garlic
1/2 cup olive oil
Juice of 1 lemon
1/2 teaspoon kosher salt
Pinch black pepper
1 pound sea scallops (10-20 per pound)

In a blender, combine basil, pine nuts, garlic, olive oil, lemon juice, salt and pepper. Blend until smooth, scraping sides with a spatula. Pesto can be made a day in advance and refrigerated.

In a bowl, combine pesto and scallops. Toss to coat evenly. Cover and marinate scallops in the refrigerator for at least 4 hours.

Heat a grill or nonstick pan to medium-high. Remove scallops from the marinade and place on the grill or in the pan. Cook until the centers just lose their translucency, about 1 minute on each side. Serve warm or chilled. SERVES 4.

Ray's Crisp Fried Calamari
WITH LEMON AÏOLI

2-3 quarts canola oil for frying
1/4 cup heavy cream
1 pound frozen calamari rings, thawed, or fresh calamari cut into rings
2 1/2 cups tempura flour
1/4 cup blackening spice
1 tablespoon ground black pepper
1 tablespoon paprika
Kosher salt

Set up a deep fryer and heat oil to 350°F.

Pour heavy cream into a large bowl. Add calamari and stir until evenly coated. Add 1/2 cup of the tempura flour and stir until the calamari is completely coated with the batter.

In a large plastic bowl with a tight-fitting lid, whisk together remaining 2 cups tempura flour, blackening spice, black pepper and paprika. Add the coated calamari to the bowl and cover with the lid. Shake bowl vigorously to coat calamari. Transfer calamari to a sieve and gently shake off excess coating. Deep-fry immediately in heated oil until golden, about 30 to 45 seconds. Using a slotted spoon, transfer calamari to a plate lined with a paper towel to drain. Season with salt to taste. Serve warm with Lemon Aïoli.

Lemon Aïoli

1 cup mayonnaise
1 1/2 tablespoons chopped garlic
2 tablespoons fresh lemon juice
1/2 tablespoon chopped fresh parsley

In a bowl, mix mayonnaise, garlic, lemon juice and parsley until well blended. SERVES 4.

Ray's owners all have their favorite foods, and for Earl Lasher, there's nothing better on a sunny day than eating a plate of Crisp Fried Calamari on the Cafe's deck.

DEEP-FRYING AT HOME

When an electric deep fryer is not available, you can still fry foods at home. Assemble the following:

4- to 6-quart heavy-bottomed, straight-sided pot

Tongs or slotted spoon

Frying thermometer

2-3 quarts oil with a high smoke point, such as canola or peanut

Fill pot with about 3 inches of oil, but not more than half full to prevent the oil from boiling over when food is added. Heat over high heat to the recommended temperature and monitor with a frying thermometer, adjusting the heat as needed. Add food in small batches and fry according to the recipe instructions. Allow the oil to heat back up to the proper temperature between batches. When finished, cool the oil completely and dispose. The oil should be used only once.

Roasted Garlic Cheesecake

WITH SUN-DRIED TOMATO–KALAMATA OLIVE RELISH

8 ounces cream cheese, softened
2 large eggs
1/2 cup Roasted Garlic Puree
1/4 cup heavy cream
1/4 cup flour
1 teaspoon lemon pepper
2 teaspoons dried thyme
1/2 teaspoon kosher salt

Preheat oven to 350°F. In the bowl of an electric mixer, beat cream cheese until smooth, about 1 minute. Add the eggs one at a time and mix until well incorporated, about 2 minutes. Add roasted garlic puree, heavy cream, flour, lemon pepper, thyme and salt, and mix well.

Spray six 4-ounce foil cups generously with vegetable spray. Fill cups 3/4 full with mixture and tap the bottoms on the counter to level the tops. Place the foil cups in a baking pan and fill the pan with hot water halfway up the sides of the cups. Cover the pan with aluminum foil and bake for 20 minutes. Remove foil and bake for an additional 20 minutes, or until a toothpick inserted in the center comes out clean. Remove cups from water bath and cool.

Turn foil cups upside down on a serving plate and remove cups. Spoon Sun-Dried Tomato–Kalamata Olive Relish beside cheesecake. Serve with crackers and flatbread.

SERVES 6.

ROASTED GARLIC PUREE:
1 cup peeled garlic cloves
1 tablespoon olive oil
1 tablespoon water

Preheat oven to 400°F. Trim off the stem ends of the garlic cloves. In an ovenproof bowl, toss with olive oil and water to coat. Cover with aluminum foil and bake until garlic is soft and golden brown, about 45 minutes. Remove from oven and mash with a fork. Cool. This can be made a day in advance and refrigerated.

Sun-Dried Tomato– Kalamata Olive Relish

2 cups julienned oil-packed sun-dried tomatoes
1/2 cup Kalamata olives, pitted and chopped
1/4 cup thinly sliced green onions
1 teaspoon chopped garlic
1 tablespoon julienned fresh basil
1/2 cup extra-virgin olive oil
Kosher salt
Freshly ground black pepper

Mix sun-dried tomatoes, olives, green onions, garlic, basil and olive oil. Season with salt and pepper to taste.

Seafood Platter
WITH THREE DIPPING SAUCES

Shaved ice
12 Pacific oysters on the half shell
8 prawns, shell on, cooked and chilled
1/2 pound mussels, steamed and chilled
2-pound whole Dungeness crab, steamed and chilled
4 ounces smoked scallops (see recipe, page 37)
8 snow crab claws, cooked and chilled

GARNISH:
Lemon wedges
Red- or green-leaf lettuce

Line a platter with shaved ice. Arrange seafood on the platter and garnish with lemon wedges and lettuce leaves. Serve with dipping sauces. SERVES 4.

The Sikma family has never determined their favorite of the three dipping sauces, but for them, the Seafood Platter is worth a rush-hour drive from the Eastside for dinner at Ray's.

NOVA SAUCE:
3/4 cup sour cream
4 teaspoons prepared horseradish
1/2 teaspoon dried dill weed
1/2 teaspoon sugar
Kosher salt
Freshly ground black pepper

In a small bowl, combine sour cream, horseradish, dill and sugar and mix well. Season with salt and pepper to taste. YIELD: 1 CUP.

RASPBERRY MIGNONETTE:
1/4 cup fresh raspberries
3/4 cup red wine vinegar
3 tablespoons minced shallots
1 teaspoon freshly cracked black pepper

Mash raspberries through a fine sieve to remove the seeds. Combine the raspberry pulp with the vinegar, shallots and black pepper and mix well. YIELD: 1 CUP.

HORSERADISH COCKTAIL SAUCE:
1/2 cup chili sauce
1/4 cup ketchup
1 tablespoon dill pickle relish
1/2 teaspoon prepared horseradish
1 teaspoon fresh lemon juice
1/4 teaspoon Worcestershire sauce
1/4 teaspoon Tabasco sauce
Kosher salt to taste
Freshly ground black pepper to taste

In a small bowl, combine chili sauce, ketchup, relish, horseradish, lemon juice, Worcestershire and Tabasco and mix well. Season with salt and pepper to taste. YIELD: 1 CUP.

FRESH SALADS AND SOUPS

Magic in the Mingling

LET IT BE SAID AT ONCE THAT THERE IS NO MYSTERY TO MAKING GOOD, PALATABLE SOUP, AND EVEN THE MORE OBTUSE AMONG US CAN TURN A FEW LEAVES OF LETTUCE INTO A CREDITABLE SALAD WITH A DASH OF OIL AND VINEGAR. BUT THE MAGIC IS in the mingling. From the beginning, Ray's always made reputable chowders and crisp mixed salads, though these were a far cry from today's upscale creations, which change with the seasons in keeping with the restaurant's embrace of the freshest of local produce and seafood. Soup stocks will start from scratch and include those imaginative elements that were, until now, known only to the chef through years of refining the brew. Today's salads incorporate intriguing greens and delicate fungi that are to be found only at specific times of the year.

This seasonal stimulation always serves to whet the diner's craving for a winter squash puree, or a rich chowder on a chilly fall night. Salads are created with fresh local albacore tuna or smoked shellfish, or enhanced by the cunning addition of fiddlehead ferns, pea vines, Walla Walla sweet onions, and other exotics to beautifully blended combinations that elevate the routine into the realm of fine dining. And the sheer abundance and enormous variety of local produce that make such choices possible—the fresh sweet cherries, blackberries, blueberries, plums and raspberries that combine into vinaigrettes and toppings; the hand-picked wild chanterelles, morels and other seasonal mushrooms that are now cherished ingredients in a variety of dishes—are as much anticipated by Ray's regulars as the vaunted seasonal runs of Copper River kings, the delectable spot prawns and the prodigal Olympia oysters that Ray's helped to reclaim.

Boathouse Salad
WITH RASPBERRY VINAIGRETTE AND CANDIED-SPICED WALNUTS

1 head butter or Bibb lettuce
1/2 cup dried cranberries
4 ounces Point Reyes blue cheese crumbles
Candied-Spiced Walnuts
Raspberry Vinaigrette

Divide lettuce onto 4 plates and top with dried cranberries, blue cheese and candied walnuts. Drizzle with raspberry vinaigrette to taste. Serve immediately. SERVES 4.

Raspberry Vinaigrette

1/2 cup red wine vinegar
3/4 cup fresh or frozen raspberries*
1 tablespoon chopped shallot
2 tablespoons honey
1 teaspoon sugar
1 teaspoon fresh lemon juice
1 1/2 teaspoons Dijon mustard
1/4 teaspoon dried thyme
1/2 teaspoon kosher salt
1/8 teaspoon freshly ground black pepper
1 teaspoon water
3/4 cup canola oil

In a 1-quart saucepan, combine vinegar, raspberries and shallots. Crush raspberries with a fork. Bring the mixture to a boil and then reduce heat to a simmer. Cook until mixture is reduced to approximately 1/4 cup, about 5 minutes. Strain through a sieve into a blender. Process until smooth. Allow to cool. Add honey, sugar, lemon juice, mustard, thyme, salt, black pepper and water. Blend until smooth. Scrape down the sides with a spatula and blend briefly to ensure that everything is well mixed. With the blender running, slowly pour in half the canola oil in a steady stream. Stop the blender and scrape down the sides again. Turn the blender on and slowly add the remaining oil, processing until emulsified.
YIELD: 1 CUP.

*If necessary, adjust the amount of sugar to taste, depending on the sweetness of the raspberries (frozen tend to be sweeter than fresh).

Candied-Spiced Walnuts

1 pound walnut halves
2/3 cup confectioners' sugar
2/3 cup granulated sugar
1/2 teaspoon kosher salt
2 teaspoons paprika
1 teaspoon cayenne pepper
2 teaspoons ground cumin

2-3 quarts canola oil for frying

Fill a 4-quart pot half full of water and bring to a boil. Add walnuts and boil until they are slightly softened, about 10 minutes. Remove from heat and drain water. In a medium bowl, combine confectioners' sugar, granulated sugar, salt, paprika, cayenne pepper and cumin. Toss walnuts in sugar mixture and set aside to dry, uncovered and unrefrigerated, overnight.

Set up a deep fryer (see page 44) and heat oil to 350°F. Deep-fry walnuts in small batches until crispy and caramel colored, about 1 to 2 minutes. Spread on a cookie sheet lined with waxed paper. Cool completely. Store in a sealed container.

Chef Ramseyer's Caesar Salad

WITH PARMESAN CRISPS

Parmigiano-Reggiano is a hard, well-aged cow's milk cheese with a lineage dating back to AD 1200. Produced in the dairy region of Cisalpine, in northern Italy, it has a rich, nutty flavor that makes it the king of Parmesans. Production is strictly controlled by the Italian government.

DRESSING:
7 anchovy fillets, chopped
2 large egg yolks
Juice of 1 lemon
1 teaspoon chopped garlic
1/2 teaspoon Worcestershire sauce
1/4 teaspoon freshly ground black pepper
1/2 cup olive oil
Kosher salt

CROUTONS:
3 tablespoons salted butter
1 teaspoon chopped garlic
1 cup bread cubes

1 head romaine lettuce, chopped
1/4 cup grated Parmigiano-Reggiano

GARNISH:
1 lemon, cut in quarters
Parmesan Crisps (see page 65)

DRESSING:

Combine anchovies, egg yolks, lemon juice, garlic, Worcestershire sauce and pepper in a blender. Process until smooth, about 1 minute. With the blender running, add olive oil in a slow, steady stream until all the oil has been incorporated. Season with salt to taste. This can be made a day in advance and refrigerated until ready to use.

CROUTONS:

Preheat oven to 350°F. In a 1-quart saucepan, melt butter over medium heat. Add garlic, stir and remove from heat. Add bread cubes and toss until butter is completely absorbed. Spread bread cubes on a cookie sheet and bake until golden brown and crispy, about 10 minutes. Croutons can be made a day in advance and kept in a sealed container until ready to use.

In a large salad bowl, combine romaine, Parmigiano-Reggiano and croutons and toss with dressing. Serve immediately with lemon wedges and Parmesan Crisps. SERVES 4.

Asian Spinach Salad
WITH HONEY-GINGER VINAIGRETTE

8 ounces spinach leaves
1/2 cup Honey-Ginger Vinaigrette
3 ounces enoki mushrooms
1/4 cup sliced almonds, toasted
1 red bell pepper, seeded and sliced
2 ounces daikon radish sprouts
1/2 cup crispy fried wonton strips

In a large mixing bowl, gently combine
spinach leaves and Honey-Ginger Vinaigrette.
Divide spinach onto 4 plates and top with
enoki mushrooms, almonds, bell pepper, daikon
radish sprouts and fried wonton strips.
Serve immediately. SERVES 4.

Honey-Ginger Vinaigrette

1 teaspoon peeled and chopped fresh ginger
1/4 teaspoon chopped garlic
1 tablespoon chopped scallion, white part only
1/8 teaspoon sambal oelek
1 tablespoon mirin
1/2 teaspoon Dijon mustard
1/2 teaspoon honey
1/4 cup seasoned rice vinegar
1 large egg yolk
1/4 teaspoon kosher salt
3/4 cup canola oil

In a medium bowl, combine ginger, garlic,
scallions, sambal oelek and mirin. Using
a handheld blender, puree mixture until smooth.
Add mustard, honey, vinegar, egg yolk and salt.
Blend until smooth. With the blender running,
slowly add the oil and blend until the dressing
is smooth and creamy. YIELD: 1 CUP.

Heirloom Tomato Salad with Buffalo Mozzarella

1 large Marvel Stripe tomato
1 German Red or Brandywine tomato
1-2 (depending on size) Orange Jubilee or Lemon Boy tomatoes
2 Green Zebra tomatoes
12 ounces buffalo mozzarella, cut into 8 1/4-inch slices
1 tablespoon sea salt
1 head baby frisée, divided into quarters
1/2 cup Basil Oil
2 tablespoons 20-year-old balsamic vinegar

8 chives, cut into 3-inch sticks

Trim the stem ends of the tomatoes and cut into 1/4-inch slices. Sprinkle tomato slices and mozzarella slices lightly with sea salt. Assemble 4 stacks by first placing a Marvel Stripe slice on each of 4 serving plates. (Note: If tomatoes are very juicy, assemble slices on a paper towel and then transfer to serving plates.) Next layer mozzarella and frisée, drizzling a small amount of Basil Oil over the greens. Layer a slice of German Red on top of the frisée, followed by another slice of mozzarella. Top stacks with 1 slice each of Orange Jubilee and Green Zebra. Drizzle the stack and plate with Basil Oil and balsamic vinegar. Garnish with chives. SERVES 4.

Basil Oil

Kosher salt
1 cup fresh basil leaves
1 cup canola oil

Fill a 2-quart pot 3/4 full of water and add 1 teaspoon kosher salt. Bring water to a rolling boil. Drop in basil leaves and stir for 10 seconds. Drain the water through a strainer and immediately place the blanched basil under cold running water. When cool, squeeze out excess water. In a blender, combine blanched basil, canola oil and kosher salt to taste. Process 4 to 5 minutes, until well combined. This can be made a day in advance and refrigerated. Shake well before using.

Feel free to try

a variety of colorful

heirloom tomatoes

available in your area.

Walla Walla Sweet Onion Salad
WITH ANCHOVY VINAIGRETTE

1 pound Walla Walla sweet onions
1 cup Anchovy Vinaigrette
2 heirloom tomatoes, such as Marvel Stripe, Brandywine or German Red
1 head frisée, quartered
1 tablespoon chopped chives

Cut onions into 1/8-inch rings. In a large bowl, combine
onions with Anchovy Vinaigrette to coat evenly. Cut tomatoes
into 6 wedges each, to yield 12 wedges. Place 3 wedges in a loose
triangle on each of 4 salad plates. Place a frisée quarter in the
center of each tomato triangle. Pile onions on top of frisée.
Garnish with chopped chives. Serve immediately. SERVES 4.

Anchovy Vinaigrette

1/4 cup white balsamic vinegar
1 teaspoon Dijon mustard
5 anchovy fillets
3/4 cup canola oil
2 teaspoons mustard seeds
2 teaspoons finely chopped chives
Kosher salt to taste
Freshly ground black pepper to taste

In a blender, combine vinegar and mustard and blend for 10 seconds.
Add anchovy fillets and blend until smooth, about 30 seconds.
With the blender running, add canola oil in a slow, steady stream
and process until emulsified. If the vinaigrette becomes too thick,
add a tablespoon or so of water as needed. Remove container from
the blender and stir in mustard seeds, chives, salt and pepper.
YIELD: ABOUT 1 CUP.

Smoked Seafood Salad

DRESSING:
1 1/2 cups mayonnaise
1/2 cup real maple syrup
1 tablespoon sambal oelek
1 teaspoon ancho chile powder
1 teaspoon smoked paprika
1 teaspoon dried thyme
1 tablespoon chopped flat-leaf parsley

SALAD:
24 clams, steamed open and chilled
24 mussels, steamed open and chilled
1/2 pound hot-smoked salmon cubes (see page 33)
1/2 pound hot-smoked scallops, cut in half (see page 37)
1/2 cup cubed roma tomatoes
8 red-leaf lettuce leaves
1/2 cup chopped flat-leaf parsley

Smoking is a wonderful way to cook and flavor seafood. See page 32 for directions.

In a medium bowl, combine mayonnaise, maple syrup, sambal oelek, ancho chile powder, smoked paprika, dried thyme and 1 tablespoon chopped parsley. Mix well.

In a large bowl, combine clams, mussels, salmon cubes, scallops, tomatoes and dressing. Toss to coat evenly. Arrange 2 lettuce leaves on each of 4 plates. Divide the seafood evenly and place on top of the lettuce. Garnish with chopped parsley.
Serve immediately. SERVES 4.

Bering Sea Red King Crab Tempura
ON A BED OF ASIAN PEAR-JICAMA SLAW WITH BLOOD ORANGE VINAIGRETTE

2-3 quarts canola oil for frying
8 4-inch-long king crab leg segments
1/2 cup buttermilk
1/2 cup tempura flour
I head baby frisée, cut into quarters

Set up a deep fryer (see page 44) and heat oil to 350°F.

Using a pair of kitchen shears, carefully snip through the back part of each crab leg shell lengthwise and pull out the meat in one whole piece. Pull out the thin strip of tendon that runs lengthwise through the center of the meat and discard. Place crab pieces in a bowl and add buttermilk, stirring to coat well. Sprinkle with 1/4 cup of the tempura flour and stir to make a wet batter. Just before frying, dust pieces with the remaining tempura flour so that the outside layer is drier. Carefully place in fryer and cook until pieces float to the top and are lightly golden, about 10 to 15 seconds.

Place frisée on each of 4 plates. Drizzle with Blood Orange Vinaigrette and top with Asian Pear-Jicama Slaw. Top each portion of slaw with 2 legs of crab tempura in a crisscross arrangement.
Serve immediately. SERVES 4.

Blood Orange Vinaigrette

2 blood oranges
1/4 cup rice wine vinegar
I teaspoon light brown sugar
I cup canola oil

With a sharp knife, carefully shave off the outer peel of 1 orange (no pith). Squeeze the oranges to yield 1/3 cup of juice. In a blender, combine orange peel, juice, vinegar and sugar. Blend until smooth. With the blender running, slowly drizzle in oil in a steady stream. Process until the vinaigrette has emulsified and looks smooth and creamy. This can be made a day in advance and refrigerated.
Stir well before serving. YIELD: 1-1/2 CUPS.

Asian Pear-Jicama Slaw

1 Asian pear, peeled and cored
1/3 pound jicama, peeled
2 teaspoons fresh lime juice
2 teaspoons olive oil
1 teaspoon rice wine vinegar
Kosher salt

Cut the pear and jicama into
thin julienne strips. In a bowl,
toss pear and jicama with lime
juice, olive oil, vinegar and
salt to taste.

Clams come in all sizes, from tiny native littlenecks to geoducks that weigh as much as 10 pounds. For chowder, some cooks prefer littlenecks or Manilas, whereas others swear by the fresh briny flavor of razor clams.

Ray's Clam Chowder

1/2 cup butter
1 pound red potatoes, cubed, skin on
1 stalk celery, diced
1/2 white onion, diced
1 carrot, diced
2/3 cup all-purpose flour
2 cups fish stock or clam broth
3 cups heavy cream
2 cups half-and-half
1/2 teaspoon Worcestershire sauce
1/4 teaspoon Tabasco sauce
1 teaspoon ground black pepper
1 tablespoon kosher salt
1 teaspoon dried thyme
1 bay leaf
14 ounces clams, chopped, with juice

GARNISH:
2 tablespoons chopped chives

Melt butter in a 5-quart stockpot over medium-high heat. Add potatoes, celery, onion and carrot and sauté for 5 minutes. Add flour and stir to make a roux. Add stock, cream, half-and-half, Worcestershire sauce, Tabasco sauce, pepper, salt, thyme and bay leaf. Bring to a boil, stirring frequently. Reduce heat and simmer until potatoes are tender, about 15 to 20 minutes. Stir in clams. Garnish with chopped chives.

SERVES UP TO 10 AS A MAIN COURSE.

Ray's Crab & Corn Chowder

1/2 cup butter
1 cup diced onion
1 cup diced red bell pepper
1 cup diced green bell pepper
1/2 cup all-purpose flour
1/2 gallon milk
4 cups corn kernels (fresh or frozen, uncooked)
3 cups diced red potatoes, skin on
1 teaspoon dried thyme
2 teaspoons kosher salt
1 1/2 teaspoons ground black pepper
12 ounces Dungeness crabmeat
1 cup cream

GARNISH:
2 tablespoons chopped chives

Melt butter in a 5-quart stockpot over medium-high heat. Add onions and sauté until translucent. Add red and green peppers. Mix in flour and stir to make a roux. Stir in milk, corn, potatoes and thyme and bring to a boil. Add salt and pepper. Reduce heat and simmer, stirring occasionally, until potatoes are soft, approximately 15 to 20 minutes. Add crabmeat and cream. Garnish with chopped chives.

SERVES UP TO 10 AS A MAIN COURSE.

Ginger Butternut Squash Soup
WITH CINNAMON ROASTED SQUASH SEEDS

3 tablespoons olive oil
1/3 cup peeled and diced fresh ginger
1/2 cup diced carrots
1/2 cup diced celery
1 cup diced onion
3 pounds butternut squash, peeled and chopped, seeds reserved
6 cups vegetable stock
Kosher salt to taste
Ground white pepper to taste
1/2 teaspoon cinnamon
1 cup heavy cream

In a 6-quart stockpot, heat oil over medium-high heat. Add ginger, carrots, celery and onion and sauté until vegetables begin to soften, stirring frequently, about 3 to 5 minutes. Add squash and stir well. Add vegetable stock and bring to a boil. Add salt, pepper and cinnamon. Reduce heat and simmer, uncovered, until vegetables are soft, about 20 minutes. Using a handheld blender or food processor, puree the mixture while slowly adding the cream. Process until smooth and velvety. This can be made a day in advance and reheated.

Ladle into serving bowls and garnish with Cinnamon Roasted Squash Seeds.
SERVES 4 TO 6.

Cinnamon Roasted Squash Seeds

Reserved squash seeds
3 cups water
1/4 teaspoon cinnamon
Pinch kosher salt

Preheat oven to 350°F. In a 2-quart pot, combine seeds and water and bring to a boil. Boil for 5 minutes. Strain the seeds in a colander and rinse with cold water to remove the pulp. Spread the seeds on paper towels and blot dry.

In a small bowl, toss the boiled seeds with cinnamon and salt. Spread in a single layer on a sheet pan lined with parchment or waxed paper. Bake until the seeds are light and crispy, about 20 minutes. These can be made a day in advance.

Smoked Tomato Soup

WITH BASIL OIL AND PARMESAN CRISPS

12 roma tomatoes
3 tablespoons olive oil
1 tablespoon minced garlic
3/4 cup chopped carrots
1/2 cup chopped celery
1/2 cup chopped onion
1/3 cup flour
4 cups vegetable stock or water
1 tablespoon tomato paste
2 tablespoons dry sherry
2 teaspoons ancho chile powder
1 teaspoon smoked paprika
1 tablespoon light brown sugar
1 teaspoon dried thyme
Kosher salt to taste
Ground white pepper to taste

Prepare a smoker using applewood chips. (See page 32 for smoking procedure.) Trim the stem ends of tomatoes. Cut in half lengthwise through the core and place cut side up on a rack in the smoker. Hot smoke until tomatoes are darkened and slightly wilted, about 30 to 40 minutes. Remove and cool. When cool, pull skins off the tomatoes. These can be made a day in advance and refrigerated.

In a 5-quart stockpot, heat olive oil over medium-high heat. Add garlic and sauté until browned, about 1 minute. Add carrots, celery and onion. Cook, stirring frequently, until the vegetables begin to soften, about 5 minutes. Reduce heat to medium and add flour. Stir to mix well. Stir in smoked tomatoes and vegetable stock. Bring soup to a boil, then reduce heat to a simmer. Add tomato paste, sherry, ancho chile powder, paprika, brown sugar, thyme, salt and pepper. Simmer, stirring occasionally, until vegetables are soft, about 25 minutes. Using a handheld blender or food processor, puree soup until smooth. This can be made a day in advance and reheated. Ladle soup into serving bowls, drizzle with Basil Oil (see page 55) and serve with Parmesan Crisps.

SERVES 4 TO 6.

Parmesan Crisps

1 cup finely shredded Parmesan cheese

Preheat oven to 350°F.
Line a baking sheet with parchment paper and grease generously with olive oil or cooking spray (or use a nonstick baking sheet or a nonstick bakeware liner such as Silpat). Sprinkle Parmesan into four ovals in a thin, lacy layer, not a thick pile. Bake until cheese is golden and bubbling, about 15 minutes. Remove from oven and, while they are still hot and pliable, carefully remove crisps from the baking sheet and drape over a rolling pin or wine bottle to shape them into a curve. Cool completely. These can be made a few hours in advance and stored at room temperature.

YIELD: 4 CRISPS.

PACIFIC NORTHWEST SHELLFISH

Variety, Volume and Versatility

THE PACIFIC NORTHWEST OFFERS SO MANY SUBTLE VARIETIES OF SHELLFISH THAT FOR THE DISCERNING DINER, THE OUTSTANDING OYSTERS, INCONCEIVABLE CLAMS AND SCALLOPS, AND MAGNIFICENT MUSSELS ARE SO UNIVERSALLY TEMPTING THAT THE selection becomes ever more challenging. Ray's makes it a little easier by doing much of the choosing, selecting Manila clams, with their sweet and tender meat and buttery nectar, or classic flat oysters related to the great Belons of France, cultivated in Dabob Bay by the oldest oyster farm in the country, Skookum and Totten Inlets, and others whose names ring like battle honors.

The tiny Olympia, the only Washington native—it's the size of a half-dollar, with a sweet, metallic ten-dollar taste—was rendered nearly extinct, originally by its popularity and more recently by pollution. Ray's effort to restore this local gem is but one of the restaurant's many contributions to Seattle's gustatory prominence. The vastly popular Pacific oyster, brought from Japan early in the last century to replace the dwindling Olympias, adapted so well to Northwest cultivation that today there are some fifty varieties with this ancestry. It is delicious cooked right in the shell over a beach fire or barbecue, and devotees will tell you it's heaven on the half-shell.

The singing pink scallop that rears its significant shell off Vancouver Island and in Puget Sound provides exquisitely flavored meat for the sagacious steamer buff, along with those tasty Manilas or choice Penn Cove mussels. And the muscle from the singing pink's larger cousin, the sea scallop, harvested off the coast here, provides meat that is outstanding in a green curry sauce and absolute perfection when house smoked and served in a chilled shellfish platter with a crisp Columbia Valley Sauvignon Blanc.

Pan-Fried Oysters
WITH HORSERADISH-APPLE SLAW AND TARTAR SAUCE

24 oysters, shucked
1/2 cup canola oil
1/2 cup butter
1 cup corn flour
2 tablespoons blackening spice
1/2 teaspoon kosher salt
1/2 teaspoon freshly ground black pepper

Drain all liquid from oysters and dry between paper towels. In a 12-inch sauté pan, heat oil and butter over medium-high heat until lightly smoking. In a bowl, mix corn flour, blackening spice, salt and pepper. Dredge oysters, one by one, in corn flour mixture to coat completely. Working in batches, fry oysters until golden, about 1 minute on each side. Transfer to a plate lined with paper towels to drain. Serve immediately with Horseradish-Apple Slaw and Tartar Sauce.

SERVES 4.

**The skilled hands
of champion
oyster-shucker
Mark Bulzomi**

Horseradish-Apple Slaw

DRESSING:
1/4 cup seasoned rice wine vinegar
1/4 cup olive oil
1/4 cup mayonnaise
1 tablespoon prepared horseradish
1/2 teaspoon sugar
1/2 teaspoon kosher salt
1/8 teaspoon freshly ground black pepper

SLAW MIX:
2 cups sliced green cabbage
1 cup sliced red cabbage
1/2 cup grated carrot
1 Granny Smith apple, peeled, cored
    and cut into julienne strips

For the dressing, combine vinegar, olive oil, mayonnaise, horseradish, sugar, salt and pepper. Mix with a handheld blender until emulsified.

In a large bowl, combine green and red cabbage, carrot and apple. Add dressing and toss to coat.

YIELD: ABOUT 4 CUPS.

Tartar Sauce

1 cup mayonnaise
1 tablespoon dill pickle relish
1 1/2 tablespoons finely chopped onion
1 teaspoon fresh lemon juice
1/2 tablespoon chopped capers
1 tablespoon finely chopped flat-leaf parsley
1/4 teaspoon celery salt

In a small bowl, combine all ingredients. Refrigerate for at least 2 hours before serving. This can be made a day in advance.

YIELD: 1 CUP.

Oysters

OYSTERS HAVE BEEN CULTIVATED AROUND THE WORLD FOR THOUSANDS OF YEARS, SOME FOR PEARLS, OTHERS FOR FLAVOR, ALL FOR ENJOYMENT. FEW LOCAL RESIDENTS KNOW, HOWEVER, THAT WASHINGTON IS THE LARGEST OYSTER PRODUCER IN THE United States. Its oyster farms ship more than 77 million pounds of Pacifics to worldwide shellfish customers each and every year.

Washington's first out-of-state market was San Francisco, where they were sent by the shipload to satisfy the Gold Rushers' craving for the tiny native Olympias found in the estuaries and inlets of Puget Sound. By the 1860s these West Coast natives had been harvested to near extinction in California waters, and new beds that were later seeded in the Bay were destroyed by superheated waters in the wake of the 1906 San Francisco quake. The rush to supply the Californians led to the dearth of these last remaining originals.

The choices at any good oyster bar at the height of the season are many, but their ancestry largely derives from the Japanese oysters brought into Puget Sound in the 1920s to replace the depleted Olympias. The hardy, mild-flavored Pacifics thrived in local waters, adapting to the variations in tidal waters, minerals and microclimates common to the bays in which they were raised—itself a complex procedure that roughly parallels the subtleties of grape cultivation for vintners. Now named for their specific home waters, oysters offer an appealing variety for aficionados to choose from, but whether they are Tottens, Hama Hamas, Skookums, Westcotts or yes—the newly revived Olympias—all are superlative examples of the grower's skill.

For some, oysters have to be cooked, whereas for purists, it's essential that they be fresh on the half shell. But baked, smoked, Rockerfellered or raw, the serving is simply a matter of taste. Whatever the option, oysters are on every gourmet's list of favorite foods.

Oyster bed on Samish Island, Washington

Fettuccine with Alaskan Weathervane Sea Scallops

3 tablespoons olive oil
24 Alaskan Weathervane sea scallops (10-20 per pound)
1 tablespoon minced garlic
2 tablespoons minced shallots
1/2 cup Sauvignon Blanc
1 cup julienned oil-packed sun-dried tomatoes
2 cups heavy cream
2 tablespoons chopped fresh parsley
Kosher salt
Freshly ground black pepper
16 ounces fettuccine, cooked al dente

In a 12-inch sauté pan, heat olive oil over medium-high heat. Pan-sear scallops, tumbling them in the pan or stirring often, until they are lightly browned on all sides, about 3 minutes. Add garlic and shallots and sauté 1 minute, stirring often to prevent sticking or burning. Deglaze the pan with wine. Add sun-dried tomatoes and cream. Reduce heat to medium and simmer, stirring occasionally, until the sauce thickens to the consistency of thin pancake batter, about 5 minutes. Add parsley and season with salt and pepper to taste. Add cooked fettuccine and toss to coat evenly. Serve immediately. SERVES 4.

Classic Clam Linguine

1/4 cup canola oil
1/2 cup finely diced red onion
1/4 cup finely diced shallots
2 tablespoons chopped garlic
1 teaspoon cracked black pepper
1 teaspoon dried oregano
1 teaspoon dried basil
1 teaspoon dried thyme
32 medium-sized fresh Manila clams
1/2 cup Sauvignon Blanc
2 tablespoons dashi
1 cup canned clams in clam juice
1/2 cup fish or chicken stock
2 tablespoons fresh lemon juice
4 tablespoons butter
16 ounces linguine, cooked al dente
Kosher salt

GARNISH:
1/4 cup freshly grated Parmesan cheese
2 tablespoons chopped fresh parsley
4 pieces toasted garlic bread

Heat a large sauté pan over medium heat and add oil. Add onions, shallots and garlic and sauté until translucent, about 2 minutes. Add pepper, oregano, basil, thyme, clams and wine. Bring to a boil and then reduce heat. Cover and simmer for 2 minutes. Add dashi, clams in juice, fish stock, lemon juice and butter. Stir to combine. Cover and bring to a boil again. Reduce heat to a simmer and cook until clams open, about 4 to 5 minutes. Add cooked linguine and toss to coat. Salt to taste.

Divide onto serving plates. Sprinkle with Parmesan and parsley. Serve with toasted garlic bread. SERVES 4.

To ensure safety, discard any shellfish that do not open when cooked.

Pan-Seared Alaskan Sea Scallops

WITH GREEN CURRY SAUCE AND MANGO PAPAYA SALSA

1/3 cup blackening spice
2/3 cup flour
2 pounds Alaskan sea scallops (8-10 per pound)
1 tablespoon canola oil
2 cups steamed jasmine rice

Mix together blackening spice and flour. Dip the flat sides of the scallops, one at a time, in the seasoned flour. Shake lightly to remove excess flour. Heat canola oil in a 12-inch nonstick pan over high heat until oil begins to smoke. Add scallops and reduce heat to medium-high. Pan-sear scallops for 2 to 3 minutes per side or to desired doneness.

To serve, place 1/2 cup steamed jasmine rice in the middle of each plate. Pour Green Curry Sauce around the rice. Top rice with Mango Papaya Salsa. Divide scallops into 4 portions and place in a circle around the rice on top of Green Curry Sauce. Serve immediately.

SERVES 4.

Green Curry Sauce

3/4 cup Thai Green Curry Paste
   (see recipe at right)
1 13.5-ounce can coconut milk
1/4 teaspoon cornstarch

In a blender, puree curry paste, coconut milk and cornstarch until smooth. Transfer to a 1-quart saucepan and heat over medium heat, whisking frequently, until sauce thickens to the consistency of heavy cream. Be careful not to boil or scorch. This can be made a day in advance and reheated.

YIELD: 2 CUPS.

THAI GREEN CURRY PASTE:

1 dried Thai chile pepper,
   or 1/2 teaspoon crushed red pepper flakes
2 tablespoons chopped shallots
2 tablespoons chopped garlic
1/3 cup peeled and chopped fresh ginger
1 stalk lemongrass, trimmed and chopped
3 tablespoons chopped cilantro
6 tablespoons canola oil
1/2 teaspoon Madras curry powder
Pinch ground coriander
Pinch ground cumin
Pinch ground cinnamon
Pinch kosher salt

In a bowl, pour 1 cup boiling water over Thai chile pepper and soak until tender. Drain. Using a food processor or handheld blender, grind rehydrated chile pepper, shallots, garlic, ginger, lemongrass and cilantro. Add 3 tablespoons of the canola oil. Process until smooth. Then add remaining oil, curry powder, coriander, cumin, cinnamon and salt and blend until smooth. This can be made a day in advance and refrigerated.

YIELD: 3/4 CUP.

Mango Papaya Salsa

1/2 ripe strawberry papaya, peeled, seeded and cut into 1/2-inch cubes
1/2 ripe mango, peeled and cut into 1/2-inch cubes
1/2 cup finely diced red bell pepper
3 tablespoons thinly sliced mint
2 tablespoons mirin
1 tablespoon fresh lime juice
1/2 jalapeño pepper, seeded and minced

Combine all ingredients in a medium bowl. Marinate for at least 2 hours. This can be made a day in advance. YIELD: 2 CUPS.

Ray's Northwest Cioppino

BROTH:

2 tablespoons olive oil
1 tablespoon chopped garlic
1 cup chopped onion
1/2 cup diced carrot
1/2 cup diced celery
1 bulb fennel, diced
1/2 cup diced red bell pepper
1/2 cup diced green bell pepper
1 tablespoon seeded and diced jalapeño pepper
1 cup Sauvignon Blanc
4 cups diced tomatoes with juice
1 cup tomato juice
4 cups fish stock
1 teaspoon saffron
1 teaspoon dried oregano
1 teaspoon dried thyme
1 teaspoon dried basil
1 bay leaf
1/4 teaspoon crushed red pepper flakes
2 teaspoons kosher salt
1 teaspoon ground black pepper

SEAFOOD:

1 pound fresh mussels, debearded
1 pound fresh clams
12 ounces salmon, cut in 1-inch pieces
12 prawns (16-20 per pound), shell off, tail on
2-pound Dungeness crab, cooked, cracked and broken
   into sections

Mussels and clams should always be alive, with the shells closed, when purchased. Buy quality shellfish from reputable fishmongers.

In a 1-gallon stockpot, heat olive oil over medium heat. Add garlic, onions, carrot and celery, and sauté until onions become translucent, about 4 minutes. Stir in fennel, bell peppers and jalapeño. Add wine, tomatoes, tomato juice, fish stock, saffron, oregano, thyme, basil, bay leaf, crushed red pepper flakes, salt and pepper. Stir. Bring to a boil, then reduce heat and simmer, covered, about 15 minutes, or until vegetables are soft. Add mussels, clams, salmon, prawns and crab and bring to a boil. Reduce heat and simmer until mussels and clams fully open, about 5 to 7 minutes. Serve immediately. SERVES 4.

Penn Cove Mussels

FOR CENTURIES, DEEP-PURPLE-SHELLED MUSSELS HAVE GROWN WILD IN COLD-WATER BAYS FROM ALASKA TO WASHINGTON. YET WHEN IT COMES TO PUGET SOUND SHELLFISH, THESE PROLIFIC MOLLUSKS HAVE BEEN THE LEAST APPRECIATED of their genre—until quite recently, that is.

In 1975, enterprising fishermen who recognized their superior flavor began growing them commercially in Penn Cove, a cold, clear reach of Puget Sound whose fresh tidal waters flow through the deep bay on the eastern side of Whidbey Island. Seeded on fiber ropes suspended in those naturally nutrient-rich waters along with their larger cousins the Mediterraneans, they mature to market size (two to three inches long) in just one year. While the bigger Meds are excellent for smoking, marinating or stuffing, the plump, sweet-tasting Penn Cove natives are superb cooked in the shell in basic broth combinations.

Up to 150 pounds of mussels cling to ropes suspended from rafts anchored in the cold, crystal-clear waters of Penn Cove, Washington. Each colony is separated, sorted by size and shipped live to markets worldwide.

Ray's chefs discovered the rich qualities of these clean, sand-free, buttery-textured Penn Coves in 1977. Firm and full of flavor, they were prepared in a simple broth and served with a hard-crusted artisan bread and local hand-crafted ales—a pairing favored by many Ray's regulars. It still is, but over the years other exceptional recipes have emerged. One favorite at Ray's steams Penn Coves in Thai spices and coconut milk, creating a nectar-rich broth perfect for dipping chunks of thick-crusted bread.

Tender and savory mussels and a glass or two of Pacific Northwest Pinot Gris? Now this is really good company!

COLD-WATER CRUSTACEANS

Northwest Nobility—Dungeness and Spots

DUNGENESS CRAB IS, AMONG THE SEATTLE FAITHFUL, AS WORTHY A DISH AS ANY MAINE LOBSTER—A CONCEPT THAT NO HIDEBOUND YANKEE WOULD EVER SWALLOW. BUT WHAT DO FOLKS AWASH IN LOBSTER KNOW ABOUT THE MAGNIFICENT CREATURE that dwells in Pacific waters from California to Alaska? For openers, it boasts the highest ratio of utterly delectable meat to total weight and is particularly potent in the Seattle reaches, where its home preparation is as much a hallowed ritual as any New England lobster boil.

Not so long ago, most restaurant proprietors considered crab too messy to deal with, and they didn't seem to understand what to do with it, either. But Ray's did. As ever, Ray's wanted the best. So rather than taking a few hundred pounds of indifferent cooked crab from a supplier, they decided to get them live and kicking and keep them happy in large live-tanks of filtered and circulated seawater. These rich-flavored crustaceans are then cooked, cracked and served. They don't come any fresher, and they don't get any better than this.

Another Ray's first, the now-ubiquitous spot prawns, were overlooked locally for years, until the early 1980s, when Russ Wohlers touched down in Loughborough Inlet, on British Columbia's remote northern coast, and met prawn fisherman Glenn Shurat, who introduced him to these delicate, sweet-flavored creatures. From then on, Wohlers regularly made the three-hour flight up from Seattle, loaded his floatplane with as many iced spots as he could legally carry, and then lumbered home to serve them in the restaurant cooked in olive oil, garlic and sea salt, just as they are today. If the noble Dungeness is the crustacean king, then the spectacular spot is assuredly the queen, and deserving of its longevity on Ray's menu.

Dungeness Crab Cakes
WITH ORANGE TARRAGON BUTTER SAUCE

1 pound cooked Dungeness crabmeat, fresh or frozen
1 1/2 cups panko bread crumbs
3 tablespoons diced red bell pepper
3 tablespoons diced shallots
3 tablespoons chopped parsley
3 tablespoons fresh lemon juice
1 tablespoon dry sherry
1/4 cup heavy cream
1 large egg
Pinch kosher salt
Pinch ground white pepper
Dash Tabasco sauce
Pinch celery salt
1/2 teaspoon paprika
4 tablespoons clarified butter or canola oil

Thaw crabmeat if frozen. Gently squeeze crabmeat to remove excess moisture, breaking up any larger pieces.

In a large bowl, mix together 3/4 cup of the panko (reserving the remaining 3/4 cup for coating), bell pepper, shallots, parsley, lemon juice, sherry, cream, egg, salt, pepper, Tabasco, celery salt and paprika. Combine thoroughly to make a batter. Add crabmeat and mix well. Divide mixture into 8 (or 12) balls. Using hands, form patties and coat with the remaining panko. Refrigerate until well chilled, about 1 hour.

In a large skillet or nonstick pan, heat clarified butter or oil over medium-high heat until it begins to smoke. Reduce heat to medium and add crab cakes. Sear until coating is golden brown and lightly crispy, about 3 to 4 minutes on each side. Add more butter or oil as needed to the pan to prevent crab cakes from sticking. Serve with Orange Tarragon Butter Sauce.

SERVES 4 AS A MAIN COURSE, 6 TO 8 AS AN APPETIZER.

Orange Tarragon Butter Sauce

1 teaspoon canola oil
2 tablespoons finely chopped shallots
1 cup Chardonnay
1 cup orange juice
1/2 cup heavy cream
2 tablespoons fresh tarragon leaves (about 5 sprigs),
   chopped, or 1 tablespoon dried tarragon
1/4 pound unsalted butter at room temperature,
   cut into small pieces
Kosher salt
Freshly ground black pepper
Light brown sugar

In a wide 2-quart sauté pan, heat oil over medium heat and sauté shallots until translucent. Add wine and orange juice. Bring mixture to a rolling boil. Reduce heat to medium and boil gently, stirring occasionally, until mixture reduces to about 3/4 cup of liquid, about 15 to 20 minutes. Add cream and bring to a boil again. Reduce heat to medium and boil gently, stirring occasionally, until about 3/4 cup liquid remains, about 10 to 12 minutes. Add tarragon and stir. Add butter a piece at a time, stirring until well incorporated. Remove from heat. Season with salt and pepper to taste. Add brown sugar a teaspoon at a time, if needed, to balance the acidity of the orange juice.
Serve immediately.

YIELD: 1 CUP.

Dungeness Crab & Rock Shrimp Cakes

WITH ANCHO CHILE MAYO

2 1/2 cups panko bread crumbs
3 tablespoons diced red bell peppers
3 tablespoons diced shallots
3 tablespoons chopped parsley
3 tablespoons lemon juice
1 tablespoon dry sherry
1/4 cup cream
1 large egg
Pinch kosher salt
Pinch ground white pepper
Dash Tabasco sauce
Pinch celery salt
1/2 teaspoon paprika
1/2 pound cooked Dungeness crabmeat, fresh or frozen
1/2 pound rock shrimp, cooked and chopped
4 tablespoons clarified butter or canola oil

In a large bowl, mix together 1 1/2 cups of the panko (reserving the remaining 1 cup for coating), red pepper, shallots, parsley, lemon juice, sherry, cream, egg, salt, pepper, Tabasco sauce, celery salt and paprika. Combine thoroughly to make a batter. Thaw crabmeat if frozen. Gently squeeze to remove excess moisture. Break up larger pieces. Add crabmeat and rock shrimp to batter and mix well. Divide mixture into 8 balls. Using your hands, form into patties and coat with the remaining panko. Refrigerate until well chilled, about 1 hour.

In a large skillet or nonstick pan, heat clarified butter or oil over medium-high heat until it begins to smoke. Reduce heat to medium and add crab cakes. Sear until coating is golden brown and lightly crispy, about 3 to 4 minutes on each side. Add butter or oil as needed to the pan to prevent sticking. Serve with Ancho Chile Mayo.

YIELD: 8 CAKES, SERVES 4.

Ancho Chile Mayo

1 dried whole ancho chile
1 red bell pepper
1 1/2 cups mayonnaise
1/2 teaspoon minced garlic
1 tablespoon lemon juice
1 teaspoon white wine vinegar
1/2 teaspoon cayenne pepper
1/2 teaspoon paprika
1 pinch white pepper
1 whole green onion, finely sliced

Soak the dried ancho chile in hot water for about 1 hour.

Broil the bell pepper in the oven or char over the flame of a gas burner until the skin is black. Place in a sealed paper or plastic bag until cool enough to touch. Remove from bag and cut pepper in half. Discard seeds and white membrane. Wash pepper under cold running water to peel off black skin, then pat dry and coarsely chop.

Remove ancho chile from water and cut in half. Discard seeds and stem. Coarsely chop chile and combine with roasted red pepper. In a blender or food processor, blend chile and red pepper for a few seconds. Add mayonnaise, garlic, lemon juice, vinegar, cayenne, paprika and white pepper. Blend well for about 20 seconds.

Pour mixture into a small serving bowl. Mix in green onion. Serve with Dungeness Crab & Rock Shrimp Cakes.

PREPARING DUNGENESS CRAB

BOILING DUNGENESS CRAB:

Fill an 8-quart or larger stockpot with water. Allow approximately 1 gallon of water per crab. Add about 1/2 cup of kosher or sea salt per gallon of water. Bring water to a boil over high heat, carefully add the live crabs one at a time and cover. After the water returns to a boil, reduce heat to medium-high, maintaining a steady boil. Cook 15 to 20 minutes, or until the crabs float to the top and the shells are bright red. Serve hot or chilled. To cool crab quickly, immediately immerse it in ice water.

STEAMING DUNGENESS CRAB:

Set up a steamer by placing a collapsible vegetable steamer basket upright inside a 3-quart or larger pot, or place a metal colander (preferably one with feet) inside the pot. Add several inches of water to the pot just to reach the bottom of the basket, and heat on high to boiling. Place live crabs in the pot and cover. Maintain a rolling boil, making sure the water does not boil dry. Steam about 20 minutes for a 2-pound crab.

CLEANING DUNGENESS CRAB:

Holding the base of the crab in one hand, place the thumb of your other hand under the edge of the shell and pry it up and off. Rinse the top shell and set aside. Remove and discard all fibrous (gills) and gelatinous parts of the body. Remove the triangular piece of shell under the crab called the "skirt" and rinse the crab thoroughly. Break the body in half, or use a large sharp knife to cut in half or quarters, as desired.

Black Pepper Dungeness Crab

SAUCE:
1 tablespoon freshly ground black pepper
3/4 cup dry sherry or rice wine
5 tablespoons soy sauce
1/4 cup oyster sauce
2 tablespoons sugar
3/4 cup chicken stock

2-pound Dungeness crab, cleaned (see page 85)
1/4 cup canola oil
4 cloves garlic, crushed
1 tablespoon cornstarch
2 tablespoons water
3 scallions, cut in 2-inch sticks

GARNISH:
1 scallion, cut in 2-inch sticks

Wrap the ground black pepper loosely in cheese-cloth and tie off with string. Place in a small saucepan and add enough cold water to cover pepper. Bring water to a boil, and boil for 10 minutes. Drain and refill saucepan with fresh water. Boil pepper again for 10 minutes. Drain and repeat process three to five times. Drain and set pepper aside to cool. This can be done a day in advance.

In a medium bowl, combine cooled boiled pepper, sherry, soy sauce, oyster sauce, sugar and chicken stock. Whisk to combine.

Traditionally, the pepper is boiled 10 times or more! Boiling releases the aroma of the pepper while reducing its spiciness. For a spicier sauce, boil fewer times. For a more aromatic sauce, boil more times.

For best flavor, the crab should be alive when cleaning. Have fishmonger secure claws with tape or elastic bands to prevent getting pinched. For the fainthearted, cook the crab first, but doing so will alter the flavor and texture.

Break the cleaned crab in half and, using a sharp knife, cut body into four portions, with two or three legs per portion. Using a meat tenderizer or the flat side of a cleaver, gently crack shells. This will allow the sauce to penetrate the meat during cooking. (Note: If using cooked crab, the meat may fall from the shell.) Reserve top shell for presentation.

In a wok or large frying pan, heat oil over high heat until lightly smoking. Add raw crab pieces and fry until they turn red, about 2 minutes. (If using cooked crab, fry about one minute.) Add crushed garlic to pan and cook until golden, about 1 minute. Add reserved top shell. Add boiled pepper sauce. Bring to a boil, reduce heat to a simmer and cover. In a small bowl, mix cornstarch and water to make a slurry. Add to simmering sauce and stir to incorporate. Cook for about 3 to 5 minutes, or until sauce begins to thicken. Add scallions. Toss crab segments to coat. Remove pan from heat. Reassemble crab segments on a plate. Pour sauce over crab. Garnish with scallions. Serve with steamed rice. SERVES 2.

Alaskan Red King Crab Legs
WITH RAY'S EMULSIFIED BUTTER

4 pounds cooked Alaskan red king crab legs

Using a sharp knife, score the backs of the crab legs to facilitate heating. In a large pot, steam or boil crab legs until just heated through, about 5 minutes. Serve immediately with Ray's Emulsified Butter. SERVES 4.

Ray's Emulsified Butter

1 pound salted butter

In a double boiler or a bowl set over a pan of simmering water (do not allow bottom of bowl to touch water), gently melt butter until it separates into three layers, about 30 minutes. Do not allow butter to boil or burn. Remove from heat. Skim the foam from the top of the butter and discard. Carefully pour the next layer, a golden liquid called clarified butter, into a separate bowl. Strain the remaining milk solids into a clean bowl. Put the bowl of milk solids back over the warm double boiler or pan of water (but do not return to heat). While whisking or using a handheld mixer, gradually drizzle the clarified butter back into the milk solids. Whisk until fluffy and emulsified. Keep warm until ready to use.

Seafood Risotto with Morels and Chanterelles

RISOTTO:
3 tablespoons olive oil
1/2 cup diced yellow onion
1/4 pound morel mushrooms, sliced
1/4 pound chanterelle mushrooms, sliced
1 teaspoon chopped garlic
2 teaspoons chopped fresh thyme
2 cups Arborio rice
1 cup Sauvignon Blanc
6 cups chicken or fish stock, simmering in a separate pot
1/2 cup freshly grated Parmesan cheese
Kosher salt
Pinch white pepper

SEAFOOD:
8 medium mussels
8 Manila clams
8 black tiger prawns (16-20 per pound), shell off, tail on
1 pound king salmon, skinned and boned, cut into 1-inch cubes
1 cup chicken or fish stock
1 cup Sauvignon Blanc

In a 4-quart saucepan, heat olive oil over medium heat. Add onions and cook, stirring, until they begin to soften, about 2 to 3 minutes. Add morels, chanterelles, garlic and thyme, and sauté for 3 to 4 minutes. Add rice and stir until all the grains are well coated. Add wine and cook, stirring, until the rice has absorbed all the liquid and is almost dry. Slowly add simmering chicken stock just until the rice is covered, but not drowning. Stir until the stock has been completely absorbed. Continue adding stock 1/2 cup at a time, making sure that each addition is completely absorbed before adding more. When all the stock has been absorbed, remove risotto from heat. Stir in Parmesan and season with salt and pepper to taste. Let risotto rest for 5 minutes.

In a 12-inch sauté pan, combine mussels, clams, prawns, salmon cubes, stock and wine. Cover and cook over medium-high heat until mussels and clams open. Remove from heat. Add the pan juices to the risotto and stir well to combine. Add seafood to risotto and toss gently. Serve immediately. SERVES 4.

Sea Salt Spot Prawns
WITH GARLIC-INFUSED OLIVE OIL, FRESH LEMON AND SAUTÉED SPINACH

1 1/2 pounds spot prawns, shell on (size varies)
6 tablespoons garlic-infused olive oil
1 tablespoon sea salt
2 lemons, cut in half

1/2 pound spinach, cleaned
Sea salt
Freshly ground black pepper

Partner Russ Wohlers discovered spot prawns on a routine floatplane flight to British Columbia— and flew back to Seattle with a full load of what was to become his favorite dish and a brand-new item on Ray's menu.

With a sharp knife, split prawns down the back through the shell and halfway into the meat. In a large sauté pan over medium-high heat, add 5 tablespoons garlic-infused olive oil and heat until smoking. Add prawns and sea salt. Sauté until the shells turn coral-red and the meat is white with no translucency in the center. Squeeze the juice from lemons into the pan and stir.

In a separate pan, heat 1 tablespoon garlic-infused olive oil over medium heat. Add spinach and stir quickly to coat evenly with oil. Cook spinach until slightly wilted, about 1 to 2 minutes. Season with salt and pepper to taste.

Divide spinach among 4 plates. Top with prawns and pan juices.
Serve immediately. SERVES 4.

Garlic-Infused Olive Oil

1 cup olive oil
2 tablespoons chopped garlic

Combine olive oil and garlic in a small pot and cook slowly over medium heat just until the garlic begins to turn golden brown, about 3 to 4 minutes. Remove from heat. Strain oil into a separate container to remove garlic.

WILD SALMON

A Northwest Legend

THE LEGENDARY CHINOOK IS CONSIDERED BY EXPERIENCED PALATES TO BE THE KING OF SALMON AMONGST ITS PACIFIC BRETHREN—THE COHO OR SILVER, RARE WHITE-MEAT CHINOOK, SOCKEYE, PINK, AND CHUM. THE LARGEST OF ITS SPECIES, the mighty king averages 20 pounds, its pink to red large-flaked meat rich in the oil and fat it stores to power its way back upriver to its spawning grounds.

In the early 1970s, even here in Salmon City, perfect fish were hard to find. Seine-caught and battered when unloaded, they were a far cry from today's "designer" fish. But like a seafood Sherlock Holmes, Ray's, armed with a wholesale dealer's license, tracked down the few fishermen supplying a handful of Seattle outlets with line-caught fish, dealing directly with suppliers who knew where to go for the best of the seasonal runs.

Ray's learned the subtle art of preparing quality salmon and quickly built the reputation for excellence that remains the restaurant's mainstay today. Currently, Executive Chef Ramseyer's salmon preparations vary with the species and the season, applying the methods best suited to each. He pairs these with his house-made fresh-fruit chutneys and remarkable sauces. These days many of Ray's sophisticated salmon eaters prefer prime Columbia River king in late winter, and perhaps the most prized (and certainly the most famous) salmon are the chinook captured as they return to their Copper River spawning grounds in Alaska in early spring. In 1983, Ray's was one of three local restaurants to introduce Copper River salmon to Seattle diners, and today the annual spring Copper River run is as eagerly awaited by gourmets nationwide as the much-touted Nouveau Beaujolais from France. For most salmonheads, in fact, it is a far more rewarding prospect.

Grilled Alaskan Coho Salmon
WITH ROASTED RED PEPPER EMULSION, CURRY OIL AND TABBOULEH COUSCOUS

4 6-ounce Alaskan coho salmon fillets, skin on
Olive oil
20-year-old balsamic vinegar

Prepare a charcoal or gas grill. Baste flesh side of fillets with olive oil and place flesh side down on grill. When marked, turn fish 90 degrees to achieve a crisscross look. Baste skin side with olive oil and turn over. Cook the fillet until the translucency is just leaving the center of the thickest part of the fillet. Total grilling time is approximately 10 minutes, depending on thickness of fish.

Place scoops of Tabbouleh Couscous in the middle of 4 serving plates. Top with salmon fillets. Drizzle Curry Oil, Roasted Red Pepper Emulsion, and balsamic vinegar around the edges. Serve immediately. SERVES 4.

Tabbouleh Couscous

1 1/2 cups uncooked couscous
1 1/2 cups cold water
2/3 cup packed roughly chopped curly parsley leaves
1 cup diced sweet onion
1 1/2 cups seeded and finely diced roma tomato
2 tablespoons fresh lemon juice
1/2 cup olive oil
1/2 teaspoon curry powder
2 teaspoons kosher salt
1/4 teaspoon ground white pepper
1/4 cup chopped fresh mint

In a medium bowl, combine couscous and water. Cover and refrigerate for 20 minutes, or until all the water has been absorbed by the couscous. Fluff couscous with a fork. Add parsley, onion, tomato, lemon juice, olive oil, curry powder, salt, pepper and mint. Mix well. YIELD: 4 CUPS.

Curry Oil

1 cup plus 2 tablespoons canola oil
1/2 Granny Smith apple, cored and chopped, skin on
1/4 cup chopped yellow onion
1 tablespoon Madras curry powder

Allow at least 24 hours of preparation time. In a 2-quart saucepan, heat 3 tablespoons of the oil over medium heat. Add apple and onion and sauté until they begin to soften. Add curry powder and mix well. Add remaining oil, heat to a simmer and cook gently for 3 minutes. Transfer mixture to a blender or food processor (be careful, it will be hot) and puree. While still hot, strain through a paper coffee filter into a bowl. Refrigerate for at least 24 hours. Carefully pour off the clear oil on top into a separate container, leaving the sediment behind. The oil can be stored in a closed container in the refrigerator for up to a month. YIELD: 3/4 CUP.

Roasted Red Pepper Emulsion

2 small or medium red bell peppers
1/2 cup olive oil
Kosher salt

To roast the peppers, broil in the oven or char over the flame of a gas burner until skins are black. Place in a paper or plastic bag and seal. When cool enough to touch, remove from bag and cut peppers in half. Discard seeds and white membrane. Wash peppers under cold running water and peel off black skin, pat dry and coarsely chop.

Puree peppers in a blender or food processor until smooth. With the machine running, add olive oil in a slow, steady stream and process until emulsified. Season with salt to taste. This can be made in advance and stored in the refrigerator for up to a week.

Grilled Copper River King Salmon
WITH PINOT NOIR SAUCE AND SAUTÉED PEA VINES

4 6-ounce Copper River king salmon fillets
Olive oil
Sautéed Pea Vines
Pinot Noir Sauce
12 blackberries

Prepare mesquite or charcoal coals. Baste flesh side of fillets with olive oil and place flesh side down on grill. When marked, turn fish 90 degrees to achieve a crisscross look. Baste skin side with olive oil and turn over. Cook just until the translucency is leaving the center of the thickest part of the fillet. Total grilling time is approximately 10 minutes, depending on thickness of fish.

Divide Sautéed Pea Vines into 4 portions and place in the center of the plates. Top with grilled salmon fillets. Drizzle Pinot Noir Sauce around the edge of each plate and garnish with blackberries. Serve immediately. SERVES 4.

Pinot Noir Sauce

1 cup Pinot Noir
6 blackberries
1 shallot, chopped
1 sprig fresh thyme
1/2 cup fish stock or chicken broth
1/4 cup heavy cream
1/2 pound unsalted butter,
    softened and cut into 1-inch pieces
Kosher salt

In a heavy 2-quart saucepan over medium heat, combine wine, blackberries, shallots, thyme and stock and reduce, stirring, until sauce is thin and glossy, about 10 to 15 minutes. Be careful not to scorch. Add cream and reduce by half, about 2 to 3 minutes. Reduce heat to low. Slowly whisk in butter one piece at a time until thoroughly incorporated. Do not boil or sauce will separate. After all the butter has been added, immediately strain through a fine-mesh sieve to remove solids. Season with salt to taste. Serve immediately.

YIELD: 1 CUP.

Sautéed Pea Vines

1 tablespoon olive oil
1/2 pound pea vines
Kosher salt
Freshly ground black pepper

In a medium sauté pan, heat oil until almost smoking. Carefully add pea vines and sauté just until vines become limp and color is bright green, about 1 to 2 minutes. Season with salt and pepper to taste.

The Kings of Copper River

FAT AND SUPREMELY FIT THEY MIGHT HAVE BEEN, BUT TO THE LOCALS, ALASKA'S COPPER RIVER KINGS WERE JUST LIKE ANY OTHER SALMON—SEINE-NETTED BY THE TON AND CANNED WITHOUT DUE CONSIDERATION OR CEREMONY. THEN IN 1983, a group of savvy Cordova fishermen realized that the prime fish that school in the mouth of the Copper River were exceptionally rich. But it wasn't until they invited a group of Seattle chefs to taste these aristocrats that the monarch was finally recognized for its truly exceptional qualities.

What began basically as a local caper is now a nationwide—even global—event, as restaurants and suppliers battle to procure the best of this gustatory sensation. The season begins in mid-May, just as the fish gather in the Copper River Flats. These kings are strong and fat-fueled for the instinct-driven 250-mile journey up the raging river to their spawning grounds 3,600 feet above in the Wrangell Mountains.

At Ray's, the arrival of the first Copper River run of the year is celebrated with a party fit for a king. The wine director selects a wide variety of regional Pinot Noirs for the occasion, and the chefs prepare this majestic maritime autocrat with the reverence it deserves.

Whether grilled, baked, poached or pan roasted, the king is treated simply, cooked quickly and served with masterly fresh-fruit and berry chutneys and regal spring vegetables that complement the full-bodied flavor of this singular Northwest native. Salmon doesn't come any fresher—or certainly any better—than this.

The headwaters of the Copper River are the spawning grounds not only for the kings, but for sockeye and coho salmon as well. The 4- to 6-pound sockeyes migrate upstream alongside kings that can weigh more than 60 pounds. They are followed across the delta by the leaner coho, which spawns in lakes and other Copper River tributaries.

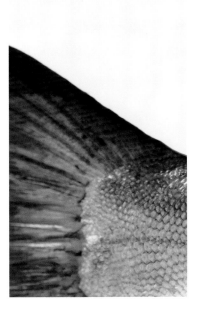

Ray's Cafe Salmon Burger
WITH BASIL MAYONNAISE AND WASABI SLAW

1 tablespoon olive oil
1/2 cup finely chopped onion
1 1/2 pounds wild salmon fillets, bones and skin removed
1 teaspoon lemon pepper seasoning
1 teaspoon granulated garlic
1/2 tablespoon kosher salt
2 teaspoons light brown sugar
4 burger rolls, toasted
Lettuce, tomato and onion
Basil Mayonnaise
Wasabi Slaw

In a medium pan, heat olive oil over medium-high heat. Add onions and sauté until golden brown. Set aside.

Grind salmon in a meat grinder or food processor. In a large bowl, combine ground salmon, sautéed onions, lemon pepper seasoning, granulated garlic, salt and brown sugar. Mix well. Cover bowl and place in the refrigerator until well chilled, about 1 hour.

Prepare a charcoal or gas grill. Divide mixture into 4 balls and press into patties. Grill over high heat about 3 to 4 minutes on each side, or until cooked through. Serve on toasted rolls with lettuce, tomato, onion, Basil Mayonnaise and Wasabi Slaw.

SERVES 4.

Basil Mayonnaise

1/2 cup mayonnaise
1 teaspoon capers
4 medium leaves fresh basil, chopped
1 teaspoon fresh lemon juice
1 teaspoon kosher salt
2 splashes Tabasco sauce

In a small bowl, combine all ingredients. Mix with a handheld blender until smooth.
YIELD: 1/2 CUP.

Wasabi Slaw

4 cups thinly sliced white cabbage
1 red bell pepper, seeded and julienned
1 yellow bell pepper, seeded and julienned
1 1/2 cups fresh bean sprouts
1/2 cup fresh French green beans (haricots), optional
4 teaspoons chopped pickled ginger
4 teaspoons seasoned rice vinegar
2 teaspoons wasabi paste
3/4 cup mayonnaise

In a large bowl, combine cabbage, bell peppers, bean sprouts, green beans and 2 teaspoons of the pickled ginger.

In a small bowl, puree remaining pickled ginger and rice vinegar with a handheld blender. Add wasabi paste and mayonnaise and blend until well mixed. Allow the mixture to rest for approximately 10 minutes.

Pour dressing over cabbage mixture and stir to combine. Refrigerate for 1/2 hour. YIELD: 5 CUPS.

Teriyaki Coho Salmon

MARINADE:
1 cup soy sauce
1/2 cup dry sherry
1/4 cup toasted sesame oil
3 tablespoons peeled and chopped fresh ginger
2 green onions, chopped
1/4 cup light brown sugar

4 6-ounce wild coho salmon fillets, skin on
Steamed rice

Allow at least 24 hours of advance preparation time.

Combine soy sauce, sherry, sesame oil, ginger, green onions and brown sugar, and mix well. The marinade should be made 24 hours in advance and refrigerated to allow flavors to blend. In a shallow glass baking dish, cover salmon fillets with marinade. Cover and marinate in the refrigerator at least 4 hours and up to 24 hours, according to how strong a flavor you prefer.

Heat grill or nonstick pan over medium-high heat. Place the fillets flesh side down on the grill or in the pan and cook for 3 minutes. Turn over and cook just until the center of the fillet becomes opaque, about 3 additional minutes. Total grilling time is approximately 6 minutes, depending on thickness of fish. Serve with steamed rice.
SERVES 4.

Teriyaki marinade is also excellent for other varieties of fish, as well as chicken and meats.

Poached King Salmon
WITH BING CHERRY CHUTNEY

Court Bouillon
4 7-ounce wild king salmon fillets

Fill a 3-quart saucepan to a depth of 11/2 inches
with court bouillon and bring to a simmer.
Carefully place salmon fillets in the liquid
and simmer, covered, until the flesh is a light
pinkish-orange and the inside is just losing its
translucency, about 4 to 5 minutes, depending
on the thickness of the fillets. Using a slotted
spatula, transfer fillets to plates and top with
Bing Cherry Chutney. SERVES 4.

COURT BOUILLON:
1 quart water
1 carrot, peeled and cut into 1/2-inch rounds
3/4 cup coarsely chopped onion
1 medium fennel bulb, coarsely chopped
1 leek, white part only, chopped
1 teaspoon black peppercorns
3 sprigs thyme
3 sprigs flat-leaf parsley
2 bay leaves
1/2 cup Sauvignon Blanc
1/4 cup white wine vinegar
1 lemon

In a large pot, combine water, carrots, onions,
fennel, leek, peppercorns, thyme, parsley and
bay leaves. Bring to a boil and then reduce to a
simmer. Add wine and vinegar. Cut lemon in half
and squeeze juice into the pot, then add lemons.
Simmer for 5 minutes. Cool, then strain. Court
bouillon can be made a day in advance.

Bing Cherry Chutney

2 tablespoons olive oil
1 small jalapeño pepper, seeded and minced
1/2 cup diced red onion
2 cups (about 1 pound) Bing cherries, pitted and halved
  (or substitute canned cherries in syrup)
1/2 cup light brown sugar
1/3 cup red wine vinegar
1/2 cup ruby port
1/2 cup water
1 tablespoon sambal oelek
1/4 teaspoon kosher salt
1/4 teaspoon freshly ground black pepper
1 tablespoon arrowroot
1/4 cup water

In a 2-quart saucepan, heat oil over medium-high heat. Add jalapeño and cook, stirring constantly, for 30 seconds. Add red onions and cook, stirring often, for 2 minutes. Add cherries and stir well. Lower heat to medium and stir in brown sugar. After the sugar has started to melt, add vinegar, port, 1/2 cup water and sambal oelek. Simmer, uncovered, for 15 minutes. Add salt and pepper. In a small bowl, combine arrowroot and 1/4 cup water to make a slurry. Stir slurry into the chutney to thicken. Remove from heat and cool. This can be made a day in advance.

YIELD: 2 CUPS.

Fresh vs. Frozen

PROCURING SUPERIOR SALMON FOR RAY'S GUESTS IN WINTER OR WHEN THE
RUNS WERE POOR WAS A CHALLENGE THAT HAD TO BE OVERCOME. ON A TRIP
TO FRANCE, RUSS WOHLERS CHANCED UPON SOME CHOICE FROZEN-AT-SEA
Pacific salmon that originated in Seattle (of all places) but was marketed mostly to
sophisticated French smokehouses. He purchased a small amount to serve in the restaurant,
where it became extremely popular. When Seattle fisherman Bruce Gore came up with
a similar idea, Ray's helped to refine his singular process into a dimension exactly right
for the restaurant.

A season of trolling the pristine waters around Sitka, Alaska, for both fresh and frozen-at-sea salmon
Photos by Dan Lamont

Gore trolls Alaskan waters for salmon at the zenith of their physical development. Once hooked, the fish are pulled one at a time to prevent bruising, quickly cleaned and flash-frozen, and kept at minus 40 degrees Fahrenheit. Tagged with Gore's Triad Fisheries label, each individual salmon is given a serial number through which every fish out of the water can be traced—when and where it was caught and precisely who caught it. "Biochemically, our fish are actually two hours fresh at the point of thaw, and it's obvious that the very freshest fish come in a frozen state—absolutely the safest, most highly monitored protein product of any kind in the world—and unmatched in flavor," states Gore. And the fact is that even some of the most astute palates in the business cannot tell this fast-frozen salmon from fresh—Julia Child's among them!

Pan-Roasted Copper River Sockeye Salmon

WITH CREAMED SWEET CORN SAUCE AND SPRING RAGOUT OF MORELS, RAMPS AND FIDDLEHEAD FERNS

4 7-ounce Copper River sockeye salmon fillets, skin on
Kosher salt
Freshly ground black pepper
2 tablespoons olive oil

Preheat oven to 350°F. Season flesh side of salmon fillets with salt and pepper to taste. Heat olive oil in a large nonstick ovenproof sauté pan over medium-high heat. Add fillets, flesh side down, and sear until a crust forms, about 3 to 4 minutes. Turn fillets over to the skin side and place the pan, uncovered, in the oven. Roast until the translucency is just leaving the center of the fillets, about 3 to 5 minutes, depending on the thickness.

Spoon the Creamed Sweet Corn Sauce in the middle of 4 plates. Top with the Spring Ragoût. Place the fish on the ragoût and serve immediately. SERVES 4.

Creamed Sweet Corn Sauce

2 ears (about 1 cup) fresh sweet corn cut from the cob, reserving cobs to make corn stock
2 tablespoons butter
1/4 cup finely chopped shallot
1 tablespoon diced red bell pepper
1/4 cup all-purpose flour
2 cups corn stock
1 cup heavy cream
1/4 teaspoon turmeric
Kosher salt to taste
1/3 cup thinly sliced basil

To make the corn stock, simmer the corn cobs in 6 cups water for 20 to 30 minutes, reducing to 2 cups of liquid. This can be done a day in advance.

In a large saucepan, melt butter over medium-low heat. Add shallots and bell pepper and sauté until soft, about 1 to 2 minutes. Add corn and cook, stirring, for another 2 minutes. Add flour and mix thoroughly to make a roux. Whisk in corn stock, stirring frequently as the sauce begins to thicken. Increase the heat to medium and add cream, turmeric and salt. Cook gently, stirring often, until it reaches a thick consistency like porridge, about 20 to 25 minutes. Remove from heat and add basil. This can be made a day in advance. SERVES 4.

Spring Ragoût of Morels, Ramps and Fiddlehead Ferns

1/2 pound fiddlehead ferns
2 tablespoons olive oil
1/2 pound fresh morel mushrooms, cut in half or quarters (if very large)
20 ramps (also known as wild leeks), ends trimmed, cut in 3-inch pieces
1/4 cup Sauvignon Blanc
Kosher salt
Freshly ground black pepper

Fill a 3-quart pot 3/4 full of water and add 1 teaspoon salt. Bring water to a rolling boil and add fiddle-head ferns. Boil for 5 minutes, stirring often. Remove ferns and immediately immerse them in a bowl of ice water to stop the cooking. Drain and set aside.

In a 12-inch sauté pan, heat olive oil over medium-high heat. Add morels and cook, stirring often, until mushrooms begin to soften, about 1 minute. Add ramps and blanched fiddlehead ferns, and cook for 3 to 4 minutes, stirring often. Add wine and deglaze pan, about 30 seconds. Vegetables should be just cooked through. Season with salt and pepper to taste. Serve immediately, using a slotted spoon to drain pan juices. SERVES 4.

Oven-Roasted Whole Coho Salmon
WITH GRANNY SMITH APPLE & DRIED CRANBERRY CHUTNEY

3- to 3 1/2-pound whole wild coho salmon, cleaned
I small bunch green onions, trimmed
1/2 cup olive oil
Kosher salt
Freshly ground black pepper

Preheat oven to 350°F. Place 2 sheets of heavy-duty aluminum foil together and coat with olive oil. Place the fish on top of the foil. Stuff the belly cavity with green onions and brush the skin with 1/2 cup olive oil. Season the skin and belly cavity with salt and pepper to taste. Bring up foil around fish, sealing tightly but leaving air space between fish and foil. Bake the fish until the flesh next to the bone has just lost its translucency, about 30 minutes. Remove the fish from the oven. Leave the skin on or remove, according to your preference. Transfer the fish to a platter and serve hot or chilled with Granny Smith Apple & Dried Cranberry Chutney. The fish can be made a day in advance and refrigerated (if serving cold). SERVES 4 TO 6.

Granny Smith Apple & Dried Cranberry Chutney

2 tablespoons olive oil
I 1/2 cups diced red onion
2 pounds (about 6) Granny Smith apples, skin on, cored and diced into 1/2-inch cubes
2 teaspoons Chinese five-spice powder
1/2 teaspoon Madras curry powder
I cup light brown sugar
1/2 cup rice wine vinegar
1/2 cup Sauvignon Blanc
3 tablespoons Major Grey's Mango Chutney
1/3 cup diced red bell pepper
1/2 cup dried cranberries
1/4 cup sliced scallion greens

Heat olive oil in a 5-quart saucepan over medium-high heat. Sauté onions until they become translucent and begin to soften. Add apples, five-spice powder and curry powder and mix well. Reduce heat to medium and add brown sugar. Stir until the sugar begins to melt and coats the apples evenly. Add vinegar, wine, chutney and bell pepper. Simmer for 15 minutes. Add dried cranberries and continue simmering for an additional 15 minutes, or until the sauce begins to thicken and the cranberries have plumped up. Remove pan from heat and let cool for 20 minutes. Stir in the scallions. This can be made a day in advance and refrigerated. YIELD: 4 CUPS.

WHITE FISH

Up from the Bottom

TIME WAS, HERE IN SALMON COUNTRY, THAT WHITE FISH IN GENERAL WERE HARDLY REGARDED AS CHOICE, AND SOME BOTTOM FISH WERE JUST BAIT, DUE PERHAPS IN PART TO THE LATE EMERGENCE OF WHITE FISH FOR SERIOUS CONSIDERATION IN THE salmon-saturated Northwest. Fortunately, more educated palates have since prevailed. Alaskan halibut, with its firm, dense big-flaked flesh, was ever a noble and prized fish, and cod, once the world's most valuable utilitarian fish, has risen to new gustatory heights. Limited here in the Pacific, it lends its name to many delightful unrelated species, the abundant and mildly flavored ling and rock cod among them.

These latter, also known as rockfish and Pacific or red snapper, never really made the right impression on the public palate until Ray's, bowing to the obvious conclusion that not all people like salmon, made white fish exciting enough on the plate to change people's minds. Indeed, if you were to ask regulars to name the restaurant's signature dish, you might be surprised to learn that the preference is not necessarily grilled wild salmon but rather black cod, marinated in sake lees, the heavy sediment thrown off in the bottle as a result of the sake-aging process.

Columbia River sturgeon—huge creatures whose magnificent flesh provides unsurpassable grilled steaks that require the simplest of treatments—are caught by locals whose families have been around the river for generations. And local albacore, while not strictly a white-meat fish, happily comes into play in July and August, and provides fabulous steaks (the meat turns white after cooking) or, when lightly seared, radically enhances summer salads.

Steamed Alaskan Ling Cod

WITH GARLIC-GINGER BLACK BEAN SAUCE

4 tablespoons salted fermented black beans
3/4 cup water
1/4 cup soy sauce
1/4 cup dry sherry
1/2 teaspoon toasted sesame oil
1 teaspoon sugar
1 teaspoon chopped fresh ginger
1 teaspoon chopped fresh garlic
4 6-ounce Alaskan ling cod fillets

In a small bowl, cover black beans with plenty of water and soak for 1 hour. Rinse well under cold running water and drain.

In a 6-inch skillet over medium-high heat, combine soaked black beans and 1/2 cup water. Cook until almost dry. Add the remaining 1/4 cup water, soy sauce, sherry, sesame oil, sugar, ginger and garlic. Bring mixture to a boil. Reduce heat to a simmer and cook until slightly thickened, about 2 minutes. Remove from heat.

Set up a steamer (see below) and heat water to simmering. Do not boil. Place ling cod fillets in a single layer in a casserole dish or individual bowls that will fit inside your steamer. Pour the black bean sauce over the fillets. Place inside the simmering steamer and cook, covered, until fillets are pearly white but still shiny throughout and break easily into large flakes. Remove bowl from steamer and serve immediately. SERVES 4.

THREE WAYS TO STEAM FISH AT HOME

1. Place a collapsible vegetable steamer basket upright inside a 3-quart saucepot. Fill pot with about 1 inch of water to just reach the bottom of the basket and heat to simmering. Place bowl or dish inside the pot on top of the basket.

2. Invert an 8-inch metal colander and place inside a 3- to 4-gallon stockpot. Add about 2 inches of water to the pot and heat to simmering. Place bowl or dish inside the pot on top of the feet of the colander.

3. Use a bamboo steamer in the traditional way.

Pecan-Crusted Petrale Sole

WITH WILTED RAINBOW CHARD, WARM FINGERLING POTATO SALAD AND CHARDONNAY PRAWN BUTTER

4 large petrale sole fillets (about 1 1/2 to 2 pounds)
Pinch paprika
Kosher salt
Freshly ground black pepper
1/2 cup pecan halves, lightly toasted and chopped
1/2 cup melted butter
1 cup Chardonnay

Preheat oven to 400°F. Fold one end of each fillet under as if you were going to stuff it. Place folded fillets on a lightly oiled roasting pan. Sprinkle with paprika and season with salt and pepper to taste. Sprinkle fillets with chopped pecans and drizzle with melted butter. Add wine to the roasting pan and roast until the translucency has left the center of the fillets, about 15 minutes, depending on the thickness of the fish. Transfer fillets to a warm platter, reserving pan juices for the Chardonnay Prawn Butter.

To serve, place Warm Fingerling Potato Salad in the center of each plate. Spoon the Wilted Rainbow Chard on top of the potato salad. Stack sole on top of the chard. Pool Chardonnay Prawn Butter around the stack. Serve immediately. SERVES 4.

Warm Fingerling Potato Salad

1 1/2 pounds fingerling potatoes,
    cut on the bias into 3/4-inch slices
1/2 cup olive oil
2 tablespoons Dijon mustard
1 tablespoon chopped chives
Kosher salt
Freshly ground black pepper

Steam potatoes, or cook gently over low heat in enough water to cover, until they are soft in the center but still hold their shape. In a bowl, combine olive oil, mustard, and chives. Add potatoes and toss to coat. Season with salt and pepper to taste. Serve warm.

Wilted Rainbow Chard

1 large bunch rainbow chard
4 tablespoons olive oil
3 cloves garlic, chopped
Kosher salt
Black pepper

Remove the stems from the chard and
cut into 1/4-inch slices. Chop the leaves
into bite-sized pieces. In a large sauté pan,
heat olive oil over medium-high heat.
Add the chard stems and cook, stirring
frequently, until they begin to soften, about
3 to 4 minutes. Add garlic and cook until
it begins to brown, about 1 to 2 minutes.
Add the chard leaves and, using tongs,
toss to mix well. Reduce heat and cook
until leaves are slightly wilted, about
2 minutes. Add salt and pepper to taste.
Serve immediately.

Chardonnay Prawn Butter

2 cups packed prawn shells
1/4 pound melted butter, hot
Reserved pan juices from the petrale sole
Kosher salt

Preheat oven to 500°F. Spread shells evenly on a lightly oiled
sheet pan. Roast until the shells turn pink and become fragrant,
about 2 minutes. Place roasted shells and hot butter in a blender
and puree until smooth, about 5 minutes (longer blending brings
out more of the pink color). Strain butter through a sieve and chill.
As the butter begins to harden, stir to re-emulsify. Chill just to the
consistency of a thick puree.

Pour pan juices into a small saucepan and heat over medium heat.
Stir in prawn butter and swirl the pan vigorously to emulsify.
Season with salt to taste. Serve immediately.

Parmesan-Crusted Halibut
WITH ROASTED TOMATO AND ARTICHOKE RAGOUT

1/2 cup flour
2 large eggs
2 tablespoons water
2 cups panko bread crumbs
1 cup shredded Parmesan cheese
Zest of 1 lemon, chopped
4 6-ounce halibut fillets, skin removed
3 tablespoons olive oil

GARNISH:
4 sprigs basil

Set up 3 bowls. Place flour in the first bowl. In the second bowl, beat eggs and water. In the third bowl, combine panko, Parmesan and chopped lemon zest. First, dredge the flesh side of halibut fillets in the flour, shaking off the excess. Next, dip the flesh side in the egg. Third, dredge the flesh side in the panko mixture to coat and then pat gently to press the mixture into the egg.

Preheat oven to 400°F. Heat olive oil in an ovenproof nonstick pan on medium-high heat. Carefully place fillets crust side down in the pan. Sear until a golden-brown crust forms, about 4 minutes. Turn fillets over and place the pan in the preheated oven. Roast until the centers are pearly white and opaque, about 3 to 5 minutes, depending on the thickness of the fillets.

To serve, divide the Roasted Tomato and Artichoke Ragoût between 4 plates. Place fillets on top and garnish with basil sprigs. Serve immediately. SERVES 4.

Roasted Tomato and Artichoke Ragoût

8 roma tomatoes
Kosher salt
Freshly ground black pepper
2 tablespoons olive oil
1 tablespoon minced fresh garlic
4 fresh artichoke hearts,
    cut into quarters
    (or substitute frozen
    or canned-in-water
    cooked artichoke hearts)
1/2 cup Sauvignon Blanc
1/4 cup fresh lemon juice
    (about 2 lemons)
1/3 cup julienned fresh basil
2 tablespoons unsalted butter,
    cut into cubes

Preheat oven to 350°F. Cut tomatoes in half lengthwise through the core. Place tomatoes cut side up on a wire rack set over a baking sheet. Season to taste with salt and pepper. Roast tomatoes until the skins shrivel, about 20 minutes. When the tomatoes have cooled, remove the skins and cut in half again.

In a 2 1/2-quart saucepan, heat oil over medium heat. Add garlic and cook, stirring, until it begins to brown, about 30 seconds. Add roasted tomatoes and artichokes and cook, stirring, for 2 minutes. Deglaze the pan with wine and add lemon juice. Simmer for 2 to 3 minutes and add basil. Reduce heat and stir in butter. When the butter has melted, remove from heat. Serve immediately.

SERVES 4.

PREPARATION FOR FRESH ARTICHOKE HEARTS:

4 artichokes
3 lemons, cut in half

Fill a large pot with cold water and add the juice of two lemons to make acidulated water. Remove the small bottom leaves from an artichoke and snap off the larger lower leaves to about 1/2 inch above the base. (A small part of the bottom of each leaf should be left on the base to become part of the heart.) Cut off the artichoke about 3/4 inch above the base. Using a sharp paring knife, carve away the tough outer leaves to reveal the tender, lighter-colored heart. With a spoon, scrape away the fuzzy choke to leave the heart clean. Immediately rub all surfaces of the heart with lemon and then submerge completely in the pot of acidulated water while you are preparing the other artichokes.

Using the same pot, bring the water with the artichokes to a boil. Reduce heat to a simmer and cook for 20 to 30 minutes, or until a skewer passes through them easily. The artichokes can be prepared a day in advance and refrigerated.

Pan-Roasted Halibut Cheeks
WITH SMOKED TOMATO COULIS AND CREAMY POLENTA

2 tablespoons olive oil
1 1/2 pounds halibut cheeks
Kosher salt
Freshly ground black pepper
1/2 cup thinly sliced basil

Preheat oven to 350°F. Heat oil in a large nonstick ovenproof sauté pan over medium-high heat. Season both sides of halibut cheeks with salt and pepper to taste. Sprinkle one side of halibut cheeks with basil and pat so that it sticks. Sear the cheeks basil side down until nicely browned, about 3 to 4 minutes. Turn the cheeks over and place pan in the oven until the flesh is firm but still juicy, about 4 to 5 minutes.

To serve, place a pool of Smoked Tomato Coulis in the centers of 4 plates. Spoon Creamy Polenta on top of the coulis. Divide halibut cheeks into 4 portions and stack on top of the polenta. Serve immediately. SERVES 4.

Smoked Tomato Coulis

2 tablespoons olive oil
1/2 tablespoon minced garlic
1/4 cup finely chopped carrot
1/2 cup finely chopped celery
1/2 cup finely chopped yellow onion
2 vine-ripened tomatoes, smoked (see page 65)
1/2 cup vegetable stock
1/4 cup Sauvignon Blanc
2 teaspoons light brown sugar
1 tablespoon tomato paste
Kosher salt
Ground white pepper

In a 3-quart saucepan, heat olive oil over medium-high heat. Add garlic and sauté, stirring, until garlic begins to brown, about 30 seconds. Lower heat to medium and add carrots, celery and onions. Cook until vegetables begin to soften, about 5 to 8 minutes. Chop the smoked tomatoes and add to vegetables. Deglaze the saucepan with vegetable stock and wine. Add brown sugar and tomato paste. Simmer gently, uncovered, for 15 minutes. Transfer sauce to a blender or food processor and blend until smooth. Season with salt and pepper to taste. Coulis can be made a day in advance and reheated to serve. YIELD: 2 CUPS.

Creamy Polenta

4 cups milk
1 tablespoon vegetable base
   (a bouillon paste available at
   specialty grocers)
1/2 teaspoon kosher salt
1/4 teaspoon ground white pepper
1 cup coarse cornmeal
1 cup freshly grated Parmesan cheese

In a 2-quart saucepan, add milk, vegetable base, salt and pepper. Heat over medium heat until almost boiling, being careful not to let it scorch. Add cornmeal in a steady stream, whisking constantly. Reduce heat to low and continue to stir until polenta starts to thicken, about 8 to 10 minutes. Remove pot from heat and let rest, covered, about 10 minutes. Remove cover and fold in Parmesan. Serve immediately.

YIELD: 4 CUPS.

Grilled Alaskan Halibut
WITH RHUBARB COMPOTE AND BALSAMIC MARINATED STRAWBERRIES

4 7-ounce halibut fillets, skin on
Olive oil

Prepare a charcoal or gas grill. Baste flesh side of fillets with olive oil and place flesh side down on grill. When marked, turn fish 90 degrees to achieve a crisscross look. Baste skin side with olive oil and turn over. Cook until the center of the fillet turns a pearly white. Total grilling time is approximately 10 minutes, depending on thickness of fish. Divide Rhubarb Compote onto 4 serving plates. Place halibut fillet on top of compote. Garnish with Balsamic Marinated Strawberries. SERVES 4.

Rhubarb Compote

3 cups diced rhubarb
1/2 cup light brown sugar
1/4 cup granulated white sugar
1/2 cup red wine vinegar
1 1/2 tablespoons fresh lemon juice
1 clove garlic, crushed
1 tablespoon peeled and finely diced fresh ginger
1/2 cup water

In a 3-quart saucepan, combine all ingredients and bring to a boil. Reduce heat and boil gently, stirring occasionally, until mixture reduces by half and becomes thick, about 30 minutes.
YIELD: 4 CUPS.

Balsamic Marinated Strawberries

1 cup halved or quartered strawberries
1 tablespoon balsamic vinegar
2 teaspoons sugar
1/8 teaspoon freshly ground black pepper

Combine all ingredients in a bowl and mix gently.
YIELD: 1 CUP.

Pan-Seared Petrale Sole
WITH LEMON CAPER BUTTER SAUCE AND FARRO PILAF

3 tablespoons olive oil
4 7-ounce petrale sole fillets
Kosher salt
Freshly ground black pepper

LEMON CAPER BUTTER SAUCE:
1/4 cup fresh lemon juice
1/4 cup Sauvignon Blanc
1 1/2 tablespoons capers
3 tablespoons cold unsalted butter, cut into thin slices
1 tablespoon chopped fresh parsley

In a 12-inch nonstick sauté pan, heat olive oil over medium-high heat. Season sole fillets with salt and pepper to taste. Place fillets in the pan and sear until they begin to brown around the edges, about 3 to 4 minutes. Turn fillets over and sear the other side for 1 minute. Carefully transfer to serving plates and keep warm.

Combine lemon juice, wine and capers in the same sauté pan. Turn the heat up to high and cook until the sauce boils vigorously. Reduce heat to medium-high and add butter, stirring or shaking the pan continuously until all the butter has melted and has emulsified into a smooth sauce. Stir in parsley and season with salt and pepper to taste. Top the fillets with the sauce and serve immediately with Farro Pilaf. SERVES 4.

Farro Pilaf

WITH BABY ARUGULA

8 ounces farro
2 tablespoons olive oil
2 cloves garlic, minced
2 shallots, finely chopped
1 small carrot, peeled and finely chopped
1 rib celery, finely chopped
1 small bulb fennel, finely chopped
1/2 cup Sauvignon Blanc
1-2 cups chicken or vegetable stock
2 cups packed baby arugula leaves, chopped
Kosher salt
Freshly ground black pepper

Fill a 3-quart stockpot half full of water and bring to a boil.
Add farro and cook over medium heat, stirring occasionally,
until al dente, about 20 minutes. Drain and set aside. Heat oil
in a 2-quart saucepan over medium heat. Add garlic, shallots,
carrot, celery and fennel. Sauté until the vegetables begin to soften.
Add wine and reduce until most of the liquid has evaporated. Add
1 cup of stock and the cooked farro. Simmer, adding more stock as
necessary, until the farro is slightly chewy and has the consistency
of risotto, about 20 minutes. Remove from heat and stir in arugula.
Season with salt and pepper to taste. Serve immediately. SERVES 4.

Cumin-Rubbed Sturgeon
WITH HEIRLOOM TOMATO VINAIGRETTE AND BLACK LENTIL CHANTERELLE RAGOUT

4 7-ounce sturgeon fillets, skin removed
1/4 cup Cumin Rub
2 tablespoons olive oil
1/2 cup diagonally sliced green onions

Preheat oven to 400°F. Dredge the flesh side of the fillets in the cumin rub. In a large ovenproof nonstick skillet, heat olive oil over medium-high heat just until smoking. Place fillets spiced side down in pan and sear until browned, about 1 to 2 minutes. Be careful not to scorch the spices, which will make them bitter. Turn fillets over and place pan in oven. Roast until the flesh is firm to the touch and just cooked through, about 5 minutes.

Spoon a pool of Heirloom Tomato Vinaigrette in center of 4 plates. Divide Black Lentil Chanterelle Ragoût (see next page) and mound on top of vinaigrette. Drape sturgeon over ragoût, spiced side up, and sprinkle with green onions. Serve immediately. SERVES 4.

CUMIN RUB:

1 tablespoon ground cumin
1 tablespoon granulated garlic
1 teaspoon Madras curry powder
2 teaspoons celery salt
1/2 teaspoon ground black pepper
1/4 teaspoon kosher salt
1/2 teaspoon sugar

In a bowl, mix all ingredients until well blended. Reserve 2 teaspoons cumin rub for Black Lentil Chanterelle Ragoût.

Heirloom Tomato Vinaigrette

1 Marvel Stripe heirloom tomato, chopped
1 tablespoon chopped shallot
1/2 cup seasoned rice wine vinegar
1/2 cup water
1 teaspoon Dijon mustard
1 cup canola oil
Kosher salt
Freshly ground black pepper

In a blender, puree tomato, shallot, vinegar, water and mustard. With the blender running, add oil in a slow, steady stream. Season with salt and pepper to taste. YIELD: ABOUT 1-1/2 CUPS.

Black Lentil Chanterelle Ragoût

3 tablespoons olive oil
1 tablespoon minced garlic
1/2 cup diced leeks
1/2 cup diced celery
1 cup diced carrot
1/2 cup diced fennel
1 cup black lentils
2 teaspoons Cumin Rub (see previous page)
4 cups vegetable stock

1/2 pound chanterelle mushrooms, sliced
1/2 teaspoon granulated garlic
1/2 teaspoon fresh thyme
1/2 teaspoon kosher salt
1/4 teaspoon ground black pepper

In a medium saucepan, heat 2 tablespoons of the olive oil over medium heat. Add garlic and cook, stirring, until garlic begins to brown, about 30 seconds. Add leeks, celery, carrots and fennel and sauté until vegetables begin to soften, about 3 to 4 minutes. Add lentils and stir. Add cumin rub and stir. Add vegetable stock and simmer until the lentils are tender, about 30 minutes.

Preheat oven to 350°F. While lentils are cooking, combine mushrooms, granulated garlic, thyme, salt and pepper in a bowl. Drizzle with remaining olive oil and mix well to coat. Spread mushrooms on a sheet pan lined with parchment paper. Roast until mushrooms begin to dry out and become a little crunchy, about 10 to 15 minutes. Be careful not to burn.

When lentils are tender, fold in roasted mushrooms.
YIELD: 4 CUPS.

Pan-Seared Columbia River Walleye Pike

WITH TOMATO–KALAMATA OLIVE RELISH

2 tablespoons olive oil
4 7-ounce Columbia River walleye pike fillets
Kosher salt
Freshly ground black pepper

Preheat oven to 350°F. In a 12-inch ovenproof nonstick sauté pan, heat oil over medium-high heat. Season flesh side of fillets with salt and pepper to taste. Place fillets flesh side down in the pan and sear until a golden crust forms, about 3 minutes. Turn fillets over and place pan in the oven. Roast until the centers of the fillets are pearly white, about 3 to 4 minutes, depending on the thickness of fillets. Place fillets on serving plates and top with Tomato–Kalamata Olive Relish.

SERVES 4.

Tomato–Kalamata Olive Relish

1 cup finely diced ripe roma tomatoes, juice and seeds removed
2 tablespoons finely chopped pitted Kalamata olives
1 tablespoon extra-virgin olive oil
1 teaspoon 20-year-old balsamic vinegar
1 tablespoon fresh lemon juice
1 tablespoon lemon zest, chopped
1 tablespoon chopped fresh basil
Kosher salt
Freshly ground black pepper

Combine tomatoes, olives, olive oil, vinegar, lemon juice, zest and basil and mix well. Season with salt and pepper to taste. Marinate for at least 2 hours before serving. This can be made a day in advance.

Ray's Boathouse Black Cod in Sake Kasu
WITH SESAME RICE CAKES AND WASABI EMULSION

2 to 2 1/2 pounds black cod fillet, skin on, cut into 4 serving pieces
1/3 cup kosher salt, more if needed

6 ounces (3/4 cup) sake kasu paste
1/3 cup sugar
3/4 cup water

Steamed choy sum
Sliced pickled ginger

Allow 48 hours for advance preparation.

Place black cod fillets skin side down in a shallow glass baking dish. Sprinkle a generous layer of salt over the fish, cover and refrigerate for 24 hours.

Rinse the salt from the fish and pat dry. Place fish skin side down in a clean dish.

Using an electric mixer, beat the kasu paste and sugar until smooth. Slowly add water and mix until incorporated. Pour the kasu mixture evenly over the fish, cover, and refrigerate for another 24 hours.

Prepare a charcoal or gas grill. When the grill is very hot, remove black cod from the marinade, allowing the excess to drip off. Grill fish until nicely browned and just cooked through, about 5 minutes per side. Transfer to individual plates. Serve with Sesame Rice Cakes, Wasabi Emulsion, steamed choy sum and pickled ginger. SERVES 4.

Sesame Rice Cakes

1 cup Japanese short-grain rice
1 1/4 cups water
2 teaspoons seasoned rice wine vinegar

1 tablespoon white sesame seeds
1 tablespoon dark sesame seeds

3 tablespoons canola oil

Place rice and water in a 2-quart saucepan and bring to a boil. Continue boiling for 1 minute, then cover pan and reduce heat to low. Simmer on low for 20 minutes. Remove from heat and stir in vinegar. Line the bottom of a 6-by-6-inch baking pan with parchment or waxed paper. Using a rubber spatula, transfer rice to the pan. Spread the rice out evenly and pack down tightly to about 3/4 to 1 inch deep. Cool rice in the refrigerator.

While the rice is cooking, lightly toast the white and dark sesame seeds in a nonstick pan over medium-high heat. Constantly stir or toss seeds until the white seeds start to become golden, about 3 to 4 minutes. Remove from heat and cool.

Preheat oven to 350°F. When the rice has cooled, carefully invert the baking pan onto a clean, flat surface. Peel parchment paper from the rice. Using a 3-inch round cookie-cutter, cut into 4 cakes. You can also cut into 4 squares or other shapes, as desired. Sprinkle cakes evenly with sesame seeds and pat lightly. In an ovenproof nonstick pan, heat canola oil over medium-high heat. Place the cakes seed side down in pan and sear until lightly browned, about 2 minutes. Turn the cakes over and bake for 3 to 4 minutes, or until heated through. Serve immediately. SERVES 4.

Wasabi Emulsion

10 tablespoons unsalted butter
3 large egg yolks
2 teaspoons pickled ginger
1 1/2 tablespoons wasabi paste
1 tablespoon rice wine vinegar
2 tablespoons warm water
Kosher salt

Melt butter in a 1-quart saucepan over medium heat, being careful not to burn. Meanwhile, combine egg yolks, ginger, wasabi paste, vinegar and water in a blender. With the blender running, slowly drizzle in the warm butter. Blend until emulsified. Season with salt to taste. Serve immediately.

YIELD: 1 CUP.

Black Cod in Sake Kasu, prepared by Chef Ramseyer, was served in New York at the James Beard House in February 2002.

Applewood-Smoked Chatham Strait Black Cod
WITH BRAISED SAVOY CABBAGE AND SERRANO PROSCIUTTO

1 cup light brown sugar
1/2 cup kosher salt
1/4 cup hot water
4 8-ounce black cod fillets, skin on

3 tablespoons olive oil

**Allow up to 6 hours
of marinating and
preparation time.**

Combine brown sugar, salt and water in a medium bowl and mix well to make a brine.
Add black cod fillets and toss to coat thoroughly. Marinate in the refrigerator for
1 hour. Remove fillets from the brine (do not rinse) and spread on a rack. Air-dry
or use a household fan to dry the fillets, turning occasionally to ensure even drying,
until the flesh is firm and the surface feels tacky, about 2 to 4 hours.

Prepare a smoker (see page 32) with applewood chips. Close the lid and heat until
the smoke seeps out thickly. Turn the heat off and place fillets skin side down on the
top rack. Close the lid and adjust the vents, or open the lid slightly, to mix in cooler
air. Smoke for 20 to 30 minutes, or until all the smoke burns out. The fillets should
not be cooked through, but rather should have a brown glaze and a subtle smoky
flavor. The smoked fillets can be pan-seared or grilled immediately or stored in
the refrigerator up to 3 days.

Preheat oven to 350°F. Heat olive oil in a nonstick ovenproof sauté pan over
medium-high heat. Place smoked fillets flesh side down in the pan and sear until
nicely browned, being careful not to burn, about 3 to 4 minutes. Turn fillets over and
place the pan in the preheated oven. Roast until the centers of the fillets are pearly
white, about 5 to 7 minutes.

Divide the braised cabbage between 4 plates and top with the black cod fillets. Serve
immediately. SERVES 4.

**This recipe is
also excellent for
smoking salmon.**

Braised Savoy Cabbage and Serrano Prosciutto

1 small to medium-sized head (about 1 pound) savoy cabbage
3 tablespoons olive oil
1 tablespoon chopped garlic
2 tablespoons chopped shallots
1/4 pound thinly sliced Serrano prosciutto, cut into 1-inch strips
1 cup chicken stock
1/2 cup dry Riesling
2 tablespoons cold unsalted butter, cut into small pieces
Kosher salt
Freshly ground black pepper

Cut cabbage into quarters and trim away the thick stem. Slice into 1/4-inch strips. In a 12-inch sauté pan, heat olive oil over medium-high heat. Add garlic and lightly brown, about 30 seconds. Add shallots and sauté, stirring, about 1 minute. Add prosciutto, cook for 1 minute and then add cabbage. Sauté, stirring constantly, until cabbage begins to wilt, about 2 to 3 minutes. Deglaze the pan with chicken stock and wine. Bring the mixture to a simmer and cook until the cabbage begins to soften, about 5 minutes. Add butter and stir until melted. Season to taste with salt and pepper. Serve immediately.

Spicy Blackened Red Rockfish

WITH CREOLE SAUCE, CORN POLENTA AND CILANTRO LIME CREAM

4 tablespoons olive oil
4 7-ounce red rockfish fillets
1/2 cup blackening spice

1 cup seeded and julienned red bell pepper
1 cup seeded and julienned green bell pepper
1 cup julienned red onion
1 cup julienned carrot

Heat 3 tablespoons of the olive oil in a large nonstick pan over medium-high heat. Sprinkle the flesh side of the rockfish fillets with blackening spice and rub. Place fillets seasoned side down in pan and sear until a nice crust forms, about 3 minutes. Turn fillets over and cook until the center of the fish turns white, about 2 minutes. Transfer fillets to a plate and keep warm until ready to serve.

In the same pan, add the remaining olive oil, red pepper, green pepper, red onion and carrot and cook until al dente. Add Creole Sauce and stir to combine.

Divide sauce among 4 plates. Spoon Corn Polenta in the middle of each plate and top with a rockfish fillet. Drizzle with Cilantro Lime Cream. Serve immediately. SERVES 4.

Blackening spice can be very potent. Use more or less according to your preference.

Creole Sauce

2 tablespoons olive oil
1 jalapeño pepper, seeded and minced
1 tablespoon chopped garlic
1/4 cup diced celery
1/4 cup diced green bell pepper
1/4 cup diced red bell pepper
1/4 cup diced red onion
1/2 cup Merlot
1/4 cup tomato paste
1 cup fish stock
2 cups canned chopped tomatoes
1/2 teaspoon paprika
1/2 teaspoon ground cumin
1/4 teaspoon cayenne pepper
1 teaspoon dried thyme
1 teaspoon dried oregano
1/2 teaspoon salt
1/4 teaspoon ground white pepper
1/4 teaspoon ground black pepper

Heat olive oil in a 3-quart saucepan over medium-high heat. Add jalapeño and cook for 1 minute. Add garlic and cook until it begins to brown, about 30 seconds. Add celery, green pepper, red pepper and onion and cook until vegetables begin to soften, about 3 to 4 minutes. Add wine to deglaze pan. In a bowl, mix tomato paste with fish stock and then add to pan. Add tomatoes, paprika, cumin, cayenne, thyme, oregano, salt, white pepper and black pepper. Bring to a boil, reduce heat and simmer until thickened. YIELD: 3 CUPS.

Corn Polenta

2 cups milk
2 cups water
1/2 cup corn kernels
1/4 cup diced red bell pepper
1/4 cup diced green bell pepper
1/2 teaspoon blackening spice
1/2 teaspoon ground cumin
1/4 teaspoon ancho chile powder
1 teaspoon salt
1/4 teaspoon ground black pepper
1 cup medium- to coarse-ground
   cornmeal

In a saucepan, combine milk, water, corn, red pepper, green pepper, blackening spice, cumin, ancho chile powder, salt and pepper. Bring to a boil over high heat. Pour in cornmeal in a steady stream while whisking to combine. Reduce heat to low and continue stirring until polenta begins to thicken, about 5 minutes. Remove from heat, cover, and let rest for about 10 minutes. YIELD: 4 CUPS.

Cilantro Lime Cream

1 cup sour cream
3 tablespoons lime juice
1/4 cup minced cilantro

In a bowl, combine sour cream, lime juice and cilantro. Mix well. YIELD: 1 CUP.

PERFECT ENDINGS

The Last Bite

THE SECRET TO A GREAT DESSERT, ACCORDING TO CHEF RAMSEYER, IS SIMPLE. "WE PREPARE OUR OWN DESSERTS FROM SCRATCH EVERY DAY." AN ESSENTIAL PROCESS, OF COURSE, FOR THOSE WHO WOULD SKIP THE ENTIRE MEAL JUST TO GET TO THE dessert and significant even for those to whom dessert is, quite literally, a trifle.

The book on compotes, crèmes, cakes, cobblers, crisps, pastries, puddings, pies, soufflés, tarts and pastries is enormous, and sometimes so daunting to even the best home cook that this essential topper to a well-rounded meal is skipped. But at Ray's, time is not a consideration. Instead, the most difficult thing about dessert is making up your mind.

Here, desserts traditionally feature Washington's superlative bounty of seasonal fruits—from local vine-ripened strawberries and raspberries to superb tree-ripened fruits from just east of the Cascade Mountains, starting in June with sweet cherries, then progressing to apricots, nectarines and peaches. Finally, as the leaves start to turn around Puget Sound, come succulent pears and crisp fresh-picked apples.

Ray's pastry chefs are encouraged to use their ingenuity and resourcefulness, and their creations are presented to the entire staff at in-house tastings where they are judged much like apple pies at county fairs. Only the best win a prized place on Ray's dessert menu.

Chefs concentrate on innovations while at the same time taking into account the dessert preferences of the guests. Among the tried-and-true favorites are the crème brûlée and white chocolate cheesecake. More classic offerings might include Wenatchee black cherry or Yakima peach crisp, or contemporary concoctions seductive enough to fire the imagination. All are delicious, but for sweet perfection try Ray's Scharffen Berger Chocolate Indulgence on for sighs.

Scharffen Berger Chocolate Indulgence
WITH SCHARFFEN BERGER CHOCOLATE GANACHE AND CHAMBORD SABAYON

1 pound Scharffen Berger bittersweet chocolate (70% cacao solids), chopped
  (Note: It is essential to the success of this recipe to use chocolate
  with 70% cacao solids.)
10 tablespoons unsalted butter
4 large eggs
1 tablespoon sugar

Fresh raspberries

Preheat oven to 350°F. Spray an 8-inch round cake pan with cooking spray and line the bottom with parchment paper.

In a double boiler, or in a stainless steel bowl set over a saucepan of simmering water (do not let the bottom of the bowl touch the water), heat chocolate and butter just until melted. Remove from heat.

In the bowl of an electric mixer fitted with the whisk attachment, whip eggs and sugar until they reach maximum volume, about 15 minutes. Eggs will be frothy and pale in color, and hold a stiff peak. Remove bowl from mixer and use a spatula to fold 1/3 of the egg mixture into the chocolate to lighten. Fold in the remaining egg mixture and stir just until combined. Do not overmix.

Pour batter into prepared cake pan and smooth the top with a spatula. Place cake pan in a large roasting pan and set in the oven. Pour enough hot water into roasting pan to come 1 inch up the sides of the cake pan. The water bath will help the cake bake evenly. Bake for 20 minutes, or until the top has a dry, matte appearance and tiny bubbles form. Remove from the oven and let cool completely. Refrigerate for 6 hours or overnight (can also be frozen until ready to serve).

To remove cake from pan, run a knife along the sides of the cake pan. Dip pan into hot water for 5 to 10 seconds. Place serving platter over the top of the cake pan and turn over. The cake should slide out. The bottom is now the top. Pour Scharffen Berger Chocolate Ganache over the cake and spread evenly with a spatula, letting it drizzle down the sides. Serve with Chambord Sabayon and fresh raspberries. SERVES 12.

Scharffen Berger Chocolate Ganache

1/2 cup heavy cream
5 ounces Scharffen Berger bittersweet (70%) chocolate, finely chopped

In a saucepan, bring heavy cream to a simmer. Place chocolate in a separate bowl and pour cream over chocolate. Stir until smooth.

Chambord Sabayon

3 large egg yolks
1/2 teaspoon vanilla extract
1/4 cup sugar
2 tablespoons Chambord liqueur
1/2 cup heavy cream

Prepare a large bowl of ice water. In a small stainless steel bowl, whisk together egg yolks, vanilla, sugar and Chambord. Set the bowl over a saucepan of simmering water (do not let the bottom of the bowl touch the water) and continue whisking until it has thickened to the consistency of pudding. Immediately place bowl in ice water and stir until cooled.

In a separate bowl, whip heavy cream to stiff peaks. Whisk into cooled egg mixture.

Deep-Dish Apple Pie

CRUST:
1 3/4 cups all-purpose flour
1/2 teaspoon salt
3/4 cup chilled shortening
4-5 tablespoons ice water

CRISP TOPPING:
3/4 cup all-purpose flour
1/4 cup + 1 tablespoon packed light brown sugar
1/4 cup + 1 tablespoon rolled oats
1/4 cup + 1 tablespoon chopped walnuts
1/4 teaspoon cinnamon
Pinch salt
4 tablespoons unsalted butter, softened

FILLING:
8 medium Granny Smith apples
1 cup all-purpose flour
1 cup granulated sugar
1 1/2 teaspoons cinnamon
1/2 teaspoon salt
4 teaspoons fresh lemon juice

GARNISH:
Vanilla ice cream
Caramel Sauce (see page 146)

CRUST:

In a mixer fitted with the paddle attachment or by hand using a pastry cutter, blend flour and salt. Add shortening and mix just until 1/2-inch pieces form. Add 4 tablespoons ice water and mix just until combined. (If the dough seems dry, add up to 1 tablespoon more ice water.) Gather the dough into a ball and flatten into a disk. Wrap in plastic and chill at least 1 hour. This can be made a day in advance.

On a lightly floured surface, roll the dough into a 12 1/2-inch circle. Spray a 10-inch deep-dish pie pan with cooking spray. Transfer dough to the pie pan and fold over the edges to be level with the top of the pan. Crimp with fingers to make a decorative edge. Chill until ready to use.

Combine flour, brown sugar, oats, walnuts, cinnamon and salt in the bowl of an electric mixer fitted with the paddle attachment. Add butter and mix until completely blended.

Preheat oven to 425°F. Peel and core apples and cut into 1/8- to 1/4-inch slices. In a large bowl, combine apples, flour, granulated sugar, cinnamon, salt and lemon juice. Spoon the filling into the unbaked crust. Spoon the crisp topping in a thin layer over the filling to cover completely. Place the pie on a cookie sheet lined with foil or parchment paper to catch drippings and bake on the lower rack for 20 minutes. Then cover the pie with foil and bake until the filling is bubbling, about 1 hour, rotating the pie 180° after 30 minutes. Remove from the oven and cool. This can be made a day in advance and refrigerated.

Serve warm with vanilla ice cream and caramel sauce, as desired.

SERVES 8 TO 10.

Almond Biscuit Shortcake with Berries

1 3/4 cups all-purpose flour
1/4 cup + 2 tablespoons sugar
1/2 cup + 1/4 cup sliced almonds
2 1/2 teaspoons baking powder
1/2 teaspoon salt
2 teaspoons almond extract
1 cup + 2 tablespoons heavy cream

GARNISH:
1 pint vanilla ice cream
Berries

Preheat oven to 425°F. In a food processor, combine flour, 1/4 cup sugar, 1/2 cup almonds, baking powder, salt and almond extract. Process just until there are no large pieces of almonds. Add 1 cup heavy cream and mix until a soft dough forms and pulls away from sides of bowl.

On a lightly floured surface, roll out dough about 1 inch thick. Cut biscuits using a 2 1/2-inch round biscuit cutter dipped in flour. Place on a baking sheet lined with parchment paper. Combine remaining dough and repeat. Brush tops of biscuits with 2 tablespoons heavy cream, top with 1/4 cup almonds, and sprinkle with 2 tablespoons sugar. Bake for 10 minutes. Reduce heat to 325°F and bake until lightly golden, about 10 minutes. Cool.

Cut biscuits in half with a serrated knife. (Note: After cutting, you can warm biscuits in oven or microwave, if desired.) Place bottom half on a plate and top with a scoop of vanilla ice cream. Spoon berries in syrup over ice cream and plate. Place top half of biscuit over ice cream and serve. YIELD: 6 INDIVIDUAL SHORTCAKES.

BERRIES:
1 pint strawberries, trimmed and sliced
1/2 pint raspberries
1/2 pint blackberries
3 tablespoons sugar

Combine strawberries, raspberries, blackberries and sugar and set aside to develop a syrup. Best if done about 30 minutes before serving.

Yakima Peach & Blackberry Crisp
WITH CARAMEL SAUCE

CARAMEL SAUCE:
1 1/2 cups sugar
1 3/4 teaspoons lemon juice
1 pint heavy cream
4 tablespoons unsalted butter

CRISP TOPPING:
1/2 cup all-purpose flour
1/4 cup packed light brown sugar
1/4 cup rolled oats
1/4 cup chopped walnuts
1/4 teaspoon cinnamon
Pinch salt
2 1/2 tablespoons unsalted butter, softened

FILLING:
2 tablespoons cornstarch
1/4 teaspoon cinnamon
1/8 teaspoon salt
1/8 teaspoon nutmeg
2 tablespoons cold water
2 pounds fresh Yakima peaches, sliced (approx. 8 cups)
6 tablespoons granulated sugar
2 cups blackberries

GARNISH:
Vanilla bean ice cream

CARAMEL SAUCE:

In a medium saucepan over medium-high heat, combine sugar and lemon juice. Swirl the pan as the sugar melts to prevent scorching. Continue swirling until the sugar is completely melted and turns a dark amber color. Protect your hands with oven mitts or pot holders. Slowly whisk cream into the melted sugar in the pan. Stir any large pieces of sugar back into the caramel over low heat until remelted. Bring the sauce to a boil, reduce heat to medium and cook, without stirring, for 5 minutes. Remove from heat and immediately stir in butter. Refrigerate until ready to use.

CRISP TOPPING:

Combine flour, brown sugar, oats, walnuts, cinnamon and salt in the bowl of an electric mixer fitted with the paddle attachment. Add butter and mix until completely blended.

FILLING:

Preheat oven to 400°F. In a small bowl, combine cornstarch, cinnamon, salt, nutmeg and water. Whisk until smooth and set aside.

Combine peaches and sugar in a large saucepan. Cook over medium-high heat, stirring frequently, until peaches are soft and the liquid from the sugar and peaches begins to boil. (Note: If the peaches are very ripe, cooking time will be minimal.) Remove pan from heat and add cornstarch mixture. Stir until the filling begins to thicken. If it does not thicken, cook over medium heat for a few minutes longer, stirring constantly. Remove from heat and gently fold in blackberries.

Spoon the filling into six 8-ounce ovenproof bowls or ramekins, or into an 81/2-by-11-inch baking pan. Spoon the crisp topping in a thin layer over filling to cover completely. Bake on the top oven rack until topping is golden brown and filling is bubbling, about 15 to 20 minutes. Serve warm with vanilla bean ice cream and caramel sauce. SERVES 6 TO 8.

Vanilla Bean Crème Brûlée

1 quart heavy cream
1 vanilla bean
10 large egg yolks
1/2 cup sugar
Pinch salt

GARNISH:
1/2 cup sugar for caramelizing tops
Fresh berries or cookies

Preheat oven to 325°F. Pour cream into a medium saucepan. With a paring knife, slice vanilla bean in half lengthwise and scrape out seeds. Add the seeds and vanilla bean to the cream. Bring the cream to a simmer and remove from heat.

In a large bowl, whisk together egg yolks, 1/2 cup sugar and salt. Slowly whisk the cream mixture into the egg mixture. Strain through a fine sieve and discard the vanilla bean.

Fill six 6-ounce ramekins with the vanilla custard and place in a large baking or roasting pan. Place the pan in the oven and fill with hot water halfway up the sides of the ramekins. Bake until set, just until the custard moves uniformly in the ramekins, about 25 to 45 minutes. (Baking time can vary widely, depending on the depth of the ramekins. For 1-inch-deep ramekins, bake approximately 25 minutes. For 2-inch-deep ramekins, bake approximately 45 minutes.) Monitor closely to avoid overbaking. Remove the ramekins from the water bath and cool in the refrigerator at least 4 hours or overnight.

Preheat broiler. Sprinkle 1/2 cup sugar in an even layer over the tops of the custards. Place ramekins on a cookie sheet and set on the top rack under broiler until the sugar caramelizes to a golden brown, about 2 to 3 minutes. (You can also use a small blowtorch to caramelize the tops.) Garnish with fresh berries or cookies. Serve immediately. SERVES 6.

Ray's Maple Pumpkin Cheesecake

CRUST:
2 cups graham cracker crumbs
2 tablespoons sugar
3 tablespoons ground pecans
4 tablespoons butter, melted

SOUR CREAM TOPPING:
1 1/4 cups sour cream
2 tablespoons packed light brown sugar

FILLING:
2 1/3 pounds cream cheese, at room temperature
1 1/3 cups packed light brown sugar
4 large eggs
14-16 ounces canned solid-pack pumpkin puree
1 teaspoon vanilla extract
2 teaspoons cinnamon
1 teaspoon ground ginger
2 teaspoons maple extract

CRUST:

Preheat oven to 375°F. Combine graham cracker crumbs, sugar, pecans and butter in a medium bowl and mix until thoroughly combined. Press mixture evenly onto the bottom of a 9-inch springform pan. Bake until lightly golden, about 7 to 10 minutes. Cool completely.

SOUR CREAM TOPPING:

Combine sour cream and brown sugar in a small bowl and mix thoroughly. Set aside in the refrigerator.

Preheat oven to 325°F. In the bowl of an electric mixer fitted with a paddle attachment, beat cream cheese and brown sugar, scraping down the sides of the bowl often, just until smooth. Do not overmix. Add eggs one at a time, beating until smooth after each addition. Remove the bowl from the mixer and stir in 1/3 of the pumpkin at a time with a spatula. Stir in vanilla, cinnamon, ginger and maple extract. Pour filling over the baked crust.

Wrap the bottom of the springform pan with foil and place in a large roasting or baking pan. Pour enough hot water into the roasting pan to come about 1 inch up the sides of the springform pan. Bake for 1 hour. Rotate pan and reduce heat to 300°F, adding water to the roasting pan if needed. Bake for an additional 1 to 1 1/2 hours, or until the center is set. Remove the cheesecake from the oven and spread the sour cream topping evenly over the top. Place the cheesecake back in the water bath and bake at 300°F until the top is set, about 10 minutes. Remove the cheesecake from the oven and roasting pan and cool completely. Refrigerate 6 hours or overnight. The cheesecake can also be frozen.

To serve, remove the cheesecake from the pan and garnish with whipped cream, as desired. SERVES 10 TO 12.

Lemon Mousse

4 tablespoons unsalted butter
3 large egg yolks
1/2 cup sugar
1/3 cup fresh lemon juice (approx. 2 large lemons)
1 cup heavy cream
Zest of 2 lemons, finely chopped

GARNISH:
1/4 cup heavy cream, whipped
1 pint blueberries

Melt butter in a double boiler, or in a stainless steel bowl set over a saucepan of simmering water. (Do not let the bottom of the bowl touch the water.) In a separate bowl, whisk yolks, sugar and lemon juice until smooth. Add egg mixture to the melted butter. Heat slowly, whisking constantly, until mixture thickens to the consistency of pudding. Strain through a fine sieve into a separate bowl and cool completely in the refrigerator.

In another bowl, whip heavy cream and lemon zest to stiff peaks. Fold into cooled egg mixture. Spoon into wineglasses or dessert bowls and chill. Garnish with a dollop of whipped cream and blueberries.

SERVES 4 TO 6.

Dinner for partner Elizabeth Gingrich is simply not complete without Ray's Lemon Mousse.

Mixed Nut Tart

1 1/2 cups flour
1/4 cup sugar
1/2 cup + 3 tablespoons cold unsalted butter
4 large egg yolks
1 teaspoon vanilla extract
1 teaspoon cold water

FILLING:
2 cups whole walnuts
3/4 cup whole hazelnuts, skins removed
3/4 cup sliced blanched almonds
1/2 cup packed light brown sugar
1/4 cup honey
2 teaspoons granulated sugar
1/2 cup unsalted butter
1/4 cup heavy cream
2 tablespoons bourbon

GARNISH:
3 ounces semisweet chocolate,
    or 1/2 cup semisweet chocolate chips

TART SHELL:

Sift flour and sugar together. Using a pastry cutter or food processor, cut in cold butter until pieces are the size of small peas. In a separate bowl, combine the yolks, vanilla and cold water. Stir into flour mixture, being careful not to overmix. Gather dough into a ball and flatten into a disk. Wrap with plastic and chill for 30 minutes.

Preheat oven to 425°F. Roll chilled dough into a 10-inch circle. Lightly press dough into an ungreased 9-inch tart pan with a removable bottom. Fold over the edge of the dough to the inside of the pan, leaving about 1/4 inch of dough above the top of the pan. Poke dough with a fork to help prevent the crust from puffing. Press dough with fingers to create a decorative edge. Bake until golden brown, about 15 minutes. Gently press down any puffed crust with the back of a spoon. Cool completely.

Preheat oven to 350°F. Spread walnuts, hazelnuts and almonds on a baking sheet and roast in the oven, stirring about halfway through baking, until golden brown, about 10 minutes. Be careful not to burn the nuts.

In a heavy saucepan, combine brown sugar, honey, granulated sugar and butter with a whisk and bring to a boil. Reduce heat to medium-high and continue cooking, stirring constantly, until mixture has caramelized, about 5 to 7 minutes. The mixture will deepen in color to a dark golden brown and pull away from the sides of the pan. Slowly stir in the cream and bourbon. (Note: Be careful! The mixture may spatter, and the steam will be very hot.) Remove from heat and stir in roasted nuts. Pour into the cooled tart shell and bake at 350°F until the top is golden and the caramel has thickened, about 7 to 10 minutes.

GARNISH:

While the tart is baking, melt the chocolate in a double boiler or in a stainless steel bowl set over a saucepan of simmering water. Do not let the bottom of the bowl touch the water. Remove the baked tart from the oven and immediately drizzle with melted chocolate in circles to garnish.

Cool on a wire rack. If you prefer a firmer filling, refrigerate the cooled tart for about 1 hour. Carefully remove from pan. Slice and serve with whipped cream if desired. SERVES 10 TO 12.

Chocolate Cake with Molten Chocolate Center

MOLTEN CHOCOLATE CENTER SAUCE:
3/4 cup half-and-half
6 ounces semisweet chocolate, chopped
1 1/2 ounces unsweetened chocolate
1/2 cup light corn syrup
3 tablespoons cocoa powder
1/4 teaspoon vanilla extract
Pinch salt

Allow at least 8 hours of preparation time.

CHOCOLATE CAKE:
8 ounces semisweet chocolate, chopped (or 1 1/3 cups chocolate chips)
8 tablespoons unsalted butter
3 large eggs
3 large egg yolks
1/2 cup + 1 tablespoon sugar
2 teaspoons vanilla extract
3/4 cup all-purpose flour

GARNISH:
Confectioners' sugar
Vanilla ice cream
Fresh berries

SAUCE:

In a heavy-bottomed 1-quart saucepan, bring half-and-half to a simmer. Turn off heat. Add semisweet and unsweetened chocolate. Whisk until melted. Whisk in corn syrup, cocoa, vanilla and salt. Turn heat back on to medium-low. Cook sauce, stirring constantly, until it has been reduced to the consistency of pudding, about 5 minutes. Remove from heat and let cool. Refrigerate sauce for 6 hours or overnight. The sauce should hold its shape when scooped with a spoon.

CAKE:

Preheat oven to 375°F. Scoop out 6 heaping tablespoonfuls of Molten Chocolate Center Sauce onto a plate and set aside in the refrigerator. Spray six 8-ounce ovenproof baking bowls or ramekins with cooking spray and place on a sheet pan.

In a double boiler or a stainless steel bowl set over a saucepan of simmering water (do not let the bottom of the bowl touch the water), melt chocolate and butter. Stir to combine and set aside.

In a large bowl, whisk together eggs, egg yolks, sugar and vanilla. Add melted chocolate to the eggs slowly while whisking. Add flour all at once and stir until just combined. Divide the batter in half and spoon the first half evenly into the 6 prepared

bowls. Bake for 10 minutes. Remove pan from oven and, working quickly, push the spoonfuls of refrigerated Molten Chocolate Center Sauce into the centers of the partially baked cakes. Top the cakes with the remaining cake batter and smooth tops with a spatula. Return bowls to the oven and bake for an additional 15 minutes, or until cakes are set and tops look dry. While cakes are still hot, carefully run a knife around the edge of each bowl and invert onto a serving plate. Sprinkle with confectioners' sugar and serve immediately with vanilla ice cream and berries. SERVES 6.

White Chocolate Cheesecake with Caramel Glaze

CARAMEL SAUCE:
1 1/2 cups sugar
1 3/4 teaspoons lemon juice
1 pint heavy cream
4 tablespoons unsalted butter

CRUST:
9-ounce box chocolate wafer cookies, crushed to crumbs
6 tablespoons unsalted butter, melted

CHEESECAKE FILLING:
3 8-ounce packages cream cheese, softened
1 1/4 cups sugar
1/2 cup heavy cream
8 ounces white chocolate, chopped
5 large eggs
1 teaspoon vanilla extract
1/4 teaspoon salt

CARAMEL SAUCE:

In a medium saucepan over medium-high heat, combine sugar and lemon juice.
Swirl the pan as the sugar melts to prevent scorching. Continue swirling until sugar
is completely melted and turns a dark amber color. Protect your hands with oven
mitts or pot holders. Slowly whisk cream into the melted sugar. Stir any large pieces
of sugar back into the caramel over low heat until remelted. Bring the sauce to a boil,
reduce heat to medium and cook for 5 minutes. Remove from heat and stir in butter.
Refrigerate until ready to use.

CRUST:

Preheat oven to 375°F. Mix together chocolate wafer crumbs and melted butter.
Press mixture onto the bottom and 1/2 inch up the sides of a 9-inch springform pan.
Bake until set, about 10 minutes. Cool completely.

Preheat oven to 325°F. Beat cream cheese and sugar with an electric mixer, scraping the bowl frequently, until smooth. Do not overmix. In a medium saucepan, bring cream to a boil. Remove saucepan from heat and add chocolate. Stir until chocolate is melted. Slowly add melted chocolate mixture to cream cheese mixture, scraping down sides of bowl, and beat until incorporated. Add eggs one at a time, beating after each addition and scraping down sides of bowl to avoid lumps. Add vanilla and salt and stir until just combined. Pour cream cheese filling over baked crust.

Wrap the bottom of the pan with foil and place in a large roasting pan. Pour enough hot water into the roasting pan to come 1 inch up the sides of the springform pan. Bake for 1 hour, then reduce heat to 300°F and bake for an additional 1 to 1 1/2 hours, or until set. Refrigerate overnight or freeze for 6 hours.

Run a knife around the inside of pan to loosen cake. Release pan sides and transfer cake to a platter. Spoon about 3/4 cup of caramel sauce on top of cheesecake and use a spatula to spread a thin, even layer. SERVES 12.

Lemon Mousse Torte
WITH MACADAMIA–GRAHAM CRACKER CRUST

CRUST:
3/4 cup macadamia nuts
1 1/4 cups graham cracker crumbs
3 tablespoons sugar
4 tablespoons unsalted butter, melted

Preheat oven to 375°F. In a food processor, chop macadamia nuts into small pieces using on/off pulses. Add graham cracker crumbs and sugar, and process until combined. Add melted butter and mix until combined. Press mixture into a 9-inch springform pan and bake until golden brown, about 12 minutes. Cool completely.

LEMON CURD:
1/4 cup sugar
9 large egg yolks, reserving 3 egg whites for the filling
1/2 cup lemon juice (4-5 lemons)
8 tablespoons cold unsalted butter, cut into pieces

In a large stainless steel bowl set over a saucepan of simmering water (do not let the bottom of the bowl touch the water), whisk together sugar, egg yolks and lemon juice until mixture thickens to a pudding-like consistency. Remove from heat and add butter. Stir until melted. Refrigerate. (Recipe continued on next page.)

1 pint heavy cream
3/4 cup sugar
3 large egg whites
2 envelopes powdered gelatin
4 tablespoons cold water
1/2 cup lemon juice (4-5 lemons)
Zest of 2 lemons
1 cup Lemon Curd (see recipe)

GARNISH:
Reserved Lemon Curd
Fresh berries

Whip heavy cream until it holds soft peaks. Set aside in refrigerator.

Don't answer the phone during this next section! Timing is critical. First, fill the bottom of a 1-quart saucepan with 1/4 inch of water and add sugar. Cook without stirring on high heat, brushing down sides of pan with water to prevent crystals forming. Monitor the temperature of the sugar syrup with a candy thermometer. When the temperature reaches 230°F, begin whipping the egg whites in the bowl of an electric mixer just until they reach stiff peaks but are still shiny, and then stop whipping. When the syrup reaches 250 to 253°F, turn the mixer back on high speed and very slowly pour the sugar syrup down the side of the mixing bowl, being careful to not let the syrup touch the beaters, or it will crystallize. Continue mixing until the meringue has cooled.

When the meringue is almost cool, dissolve powdered gelatin in 4 tablespoons cold water for 1 minute. Whisk together gelatin mixture and lemon juice in a large stainless steel bowl set over a saucepan of simmering water (do not let the bottom of the bowl touch the water) just until gelatin has melted, about 30 seconds. Remove from heat. Add zest and 1 cup lemon curd, reserving the remaining lemon curd for the top of the finished mousse. Whisk to combine.

Remove cooled meringue from the mixer and whisk into the gelatin mixture until well combined. Next, fold in whipped cream with a spatula until just combined. Pour mixture over the cooled baked crust. Freeze at least 6 hours or overnight.

Wrap a hot towel around the outside of the cake ring for a few seconds to release it. Remove cake ring and spread a thin layer of reserved lemon curd over the mousse with a spatula (best done while still frozen). Thaw in refrigerator for about 3 hours before serving. Garnish with fresh berries. SERVES 12.

Double Chocolate Walnut Brownies

1/2 pound unsalted butter
1/2 pound semisweet chocolate
3 ounces unsweetened chocolate
3 large eggs
1 1/2 teaspoons vanilla extract
1 tablespoon coffee extract (substitute espresso
  or very strong coffee for a lighter coffee flavor)
1 cup + 2 tablespoons sugar
1/2 cup + 2 tablespoons all-purpose flour
1 1/2 teaspoons baking powder
1/2 teaspoon salt
1 cup walnut halves
3/4 cup semisweet chocolate chips

Preheat oven to 375°F. Lightly grease a 9-by-13-inch baking pan with cooking spray or butter and line the bottom with parchment paper. Grease the parchment.

Combine butter, semisweet chocolate and unsweetened chocolate in a double boiler, or in a stainless steel bowl set over a saucepan of simmering water. Do not let the bottom of the bowl touch the water. Stir until just melted and set aside.

In a large mixing bowl, whisk together eggs, vanilla, coffee extract and sugar. Slowly whisk melted chocolate mixture into egg mixture.

In a separate bowl, sift together flour, baking powder and salt. Add sifted dry ingredients all at once to melted chocolate mixture and stir just until combined. Stir in walnut halves and chocolate chips.

Pour batter into prepared pan and bake for 10 minutes. Turn oven down to 350°F and rotate pan. Bake for 10 minutes. Again, reduce oven temperature to 325°F and rotate pan. Bake for 10 additional minutes (total of 30 minutes baking time). Remove from oven and cool completely. Cover and refrigerate brownies for 2 hours. These can also be frozen until ready to serve.

To serve, cut into 16 rectangles. If desired, heat and serve with a scoop of your favorite ice cream. YIELD: 16 BROWNIES.

NORTHWEST WINE CELLAR

Talking to the Chandelier

SOME WINES DEMAND FOOD, OTHERS JUST NEED GOOD COMPANY, AND KNOWING WHICH IS WHICH IS FUNDAMENTAL FOR THE ULTIMATE ENJOYMENT OF BOTH. FOR THOSE AMONG US WHOSE FAMILIARITY WITH WINE IS SCANT, A GOOD SOMMELIER IS indispensable, although Ray's has preferred the designation "wine director" ever since the indelible occasion when a guest asked if he could speak to the "chandelier." Jeff Prather, Ray's wine director for seven memorable years, was the very essence of diplomacy when he approached the diner and said, with all the dignity of a Jeeves, "I'm the chandelier, sir. How may I be of help?"

Choosing a wine should never be a test, and never has been at Ray's, where the initial concept was to make wine an accessible and meaningful part of the dining experience. By the 1980s, the restaurant's renown had spread, and Washington's vintners quickly picked up on the powerful showcase the Boathouse provided for their products. Winemakers ranging from local giant Chateau Ste. Michelle to tiny producers like Woodward Canyon and Leonetti in Walla Walla soon found their finer vintages on Ray's burgeoning wine list, and the endemic acclaim that rapidly spread beyond the region's boundaries helped build Washington into the second-largest wine-producing state in the nation. Today, Ray's cellar contains some of the best in the world. The challenge for the sommelier is to know the character of each, to offer appropriate choices for the restaurant's guests, and to act as a mentor for both diners and staffers alike. Since the servers are the diners' first contact with the wine list, they must be able to offer sound advice on what patrons might choose to accompany their menu selections. If guests remain undecided, however, they need only to call for the "chandelier" to brighten their path to wine perfection. Cheers!

GUIDE TO SPECIAL INGREDIENTS

ALASKAN WEATHERVANE SCALLOPS

Less than 500 tons of these large sea scallops are harvested annually. They therefore fetch a higher price, since their delicious cream- or tan-colored meat is rare and much in demand. Weathervanes are shucked and frozen immediately on hauling because of the long journey to distant distribution centers and because, unlike other bivalves, they cannot clamp their shells tight, and so they lose body moisture and die.

ANCHO CHILE

This reddish-brown dried chile pepper—called a *poblano* when still fresh and green—has a relatively mild, lightly fruity flavor. It is also available in powder form.

BERING SEA RED KING CRAB

This giant crustacean measures up to 10 feet across its claws and weighs as much as 20 pounds. Its white, red-fringed meat is highly valued around the globe. Although it is plentiful in Alaskan waters, the catch is now severely limited to ensure a sustainable harvest.

BLACKENING SPICE

This Cajun-style mixture contains oregano, paprika, salt, black pepper, cayenne pepper and other spices. It provides a flavorful coating and seals in juices during cooking.

CHANTERELLE

Sought after for its exquisite nutty flavor and pleasantly chewy texture, this luscious yellow- to orange-colored wild mushroom flourishes in the fall on the forest floors of the Pacific Northwest.

CHATHAM STRAIT BLACK COD

This superlative sablefish is found in the cold, deep waters of Alaska. Its mild white meat has a high fat content, which makes it ideal for smoking. Because its harvest is carefully monitored, it is available year-round in limited quantities.

DASHI

A Japanese fish stock that is usually made from kelp and bonito flakes, dashi can be found in convenient powder form at Asian food markets.

DUNGENESS CRAB

Found from Alaska to Baja California, it is the Pacific Coast's great contribution to crustacean perfection. Weighing from one to four pounds, it boasts the highest ratio of delectable pink-white meat to total weight. Superb right out of the shell, it is equally palatable in salads—and the key to perfect crab cakes.

FARRO

Also known as spelt, this cereal grain was first harvested in Mesopotamia some 7,000 years ago. Long a staple in parts of northern Italy, it has recently become popular in American restaurants and home kitchens because of its high protein content and nutty flavor. Farro is available in flour and kernel form at specialty food stores.

FIDDLEHEAD FERNS

As the name implies, these tightly coiled young fern tips resemble the carved neck of a violin. The rich green shoots stay coiled and edible for about two weeks before they emerge into fronds. Delicious steamed or sautéed, they're plentiful in specialty markets in spring and early summer. Buy fiddleheads only from reputable sources, as the wrong kind can be toxic.

FRISÉE

A mildly bitter member of the chicory family, this curly yellow- to white-leaved endive gets better as it gets older and is often used to great effect in salad mixes.

HALIBUT

This great white fish, whose superior, mildly flavored, dense meat is preferred by many contemporary diners, has become so popular in recent years that the harvest is now restricted. A carefully regulated fishing season is monitored by U.S. and international agencies to ensure limited quantities.

HEIRLOOM TOMATOES

These ancient varieties of tomatoes are grown from seeds that have not been genetically modified or mass-cultivated for color or shelf life. Heirloom tomatoes often sport unusual colors and stripes, but they are valued more for their flavor and texture than their beauty. Although not widely available, they can be found in some specialty produce markets and farmer's markets.

MADRAS CURRY POWDER

An East Indian spice mixture that varies widely from chef to chef, this is an aromatic blend of coriander, cardamom, cumin, black pepper, turmeric, chile pepper, salt and other spices. It's best when the spices are freshly ground.

MAJOR GREY'S MANGO CHUTNEY

This mango-based condiment, thought to be named for a fictitious character, is a sweet and spicy complement to many foods.

MIGNONETTE

This traditional European sauce or oyster dip is made from red wine vinegar, cracked black peppercorns, and finely chopped shallots. There are many variations, but a basic preparation is 1 cup of vinegar, 1 teaspoon of coarsely cracked black pepper, and half of a small shallot.

MIRIN

A sweet, golden low-alcohol rice wine that is used as a sweetener, this can be found in Asian food markets.

MOREL

A fabulous, expensive wild mushroom that belongs to the same genus as the coveted truffle, the morel is usually found after the rains begin in areas blackened by forest fires. Its smoky, nut-like flavor is in steady demand at *haute cuisine* restaurants worldwide—and rarity boosts its value (morel hunters are so protective of their secret sites that they often arm themselves to ward off interlopers). Morels are available from April through June.

PANKO

A coarser and lighter variety of wheat bread crumbs, panko is used by the Japanese to coat foods before frying, for a wonderfully crisp crust. It's available in specialty food stores and Asian markets.

PEA VINES

Also known as pea shoots, pea vines are the choice leaves and tendrils of pea plants. Shoots are typically harvested from snow pea vines, although they can be from any garden-variety pea. Look for them at your local farmer's market in spring and early summer. Their season is rather short, as peas do not grow well when daytime temperatures rise above 65°F.

PENN COVE MUSSELS

These magnificent plump, purple-shelled specimens, unsurpassed in flavor, are native to northern Pacific waters, especially Puget Sound, where they are farm-raised. They are suspended from fiber ropes, a process that prevents them from touching bottom, leaving them free of sand and grit.

PINK "SINGING" SCALLOPS

Once overlooked as commercially inferior in terms of Puget Sound's shellfish bounty, these tasty scallops have finally come into their own. Harvested individually by divers, they are sold live and are delicious served as steamers.

RAMP

A wild onion that looks like a broad-leaved scallion, this is also known as wild leek. Look for it in specialty produce markets from March to June.

SAKE KASU PASTE

Made from the lees of sake (akin to the sediment found in aged wines), this can be found in Asian markets and specialty stores.

SAMBAL OELEK

This potent Asian chili paste can be found in specialty food stores and many supermarkets.

SCHARFFEN BERGER CHOCOLATE

Scharffen Berger is a boutique Berkeley, California, chocolate-maker that produces exceptionally fine semisweet (62 percent cacao), bittersweet (70 percent cacao) and unsweetened chocolate (99 percent cacao) for baking and eating. Scharffen Berger chocolate is available in specialty food stores, or online at www.scharffenberger.com.

SMOKED PAPRIKA

This is the Spanish version of paprika, in which the peppers are smoked slowly over oak before being ground into powder.

WALLA WALLA SWEET ONION

Walla Walla's golden pride, named for this pretty Eastern Washington town, is found in local markets from June to September. Onions without tears, they are eaten like apples by enthusiasts. They do not store well, but Maui, Texas, and other sweet onion varieties can be substituted when Walla Wallas are not in season.

WALLEYE PIKE

This local favorite was introduced to the Columbia River from the Mississippi River system during the last century as a sport fish. It is abundant in the large reservoirs behind Columbia River dams, and can mature to weights of 20 pounds. Often underrated, it has sweet white meat that is firmly flaked and very flavorful. It is available fresh from commercial fishmongers in fall and winter.

WASABI

This is the Japanese version of horseradish, used to make a zesty condiment known for its torrid taste. It is available in both powder and paste form.

ACKNOWLEDGMENTS

AS WITH ANY GOOD RECIPE, THE SECRET TO THIS BOOK'S QUALITY IS THE RIGHT MIX OF INGREDIENTS—IN SUM, THE TALENT OF THE PEOPLE INVOLVED. MOUTHWATERING RECIPES FROM EXECUTIVE CHEF CHARLES RAMSEYER AND RAY'S CHEF STAFF WERE seasoned with the descriptive powers of wordsmith Ken Gouldthorpe, imaginatively photographed by Angie Norwood Browne, and blended with the sensitive graphic design skills of Nancy Gellos. The entire process was guided by Ray's cookbook team: General Manager Maureen "Mo" Shaw, Manager Cindy Howard, Marketing Coordinator Lori Magaro, and Charles Ramseyer himself. Beyond content, they gave this book spirit.

The process was complex. Ramseyer and Ray's culinary staff, including chefs Peter Birk and Mark Chambers, facilitated the selection of recipes, then painstakingly converted them for preparation in home kitchens. A volunteer group of employees tested each of the recipes in their own kitchens and reported back with detailed notes and comments. Some were accepted, others were rewritten and home-cooked again. The ingredients and cooking instructions were sharpened and tested yet again, this time by Ray's senior chefs, and served to a few very fortunate guests for final evaluation.

Angie Norwood Browne's tantalizing food photography reflected her understanding of food and film. She was assisted by accomplished food stylist Patty Wittmann and graphic designer Nancy Gellos, whose page layouts set the tone for the book as vividly as Browne's and Wittmann's presentations on the plate. Additional photographs were taken by photojournalist Jaimie Trueblood. From the last light on the deck to the hustle and bustle in the kitchen, his images captured Ray's unique sense of place.

Guided by his well-honed reporting talents, writer Ken Gouldthorpe gathered impressions of Ray's from its owners, employees, longtime guests, food critics, fishermen and other suppliers, and to their perspectives he added his own observations as a Ray's regular of some 24 years' standing.

Recipes and text appear deceptively simple, but accuracy in a cookbook is crucial. The daunting task of editing this book was gracefully undertaken and skillfully completed by Judy Gouldthorpe, and for Ray's by Lori Magaro.

Finally, none of this could have happened without the total and characteristically enthusiastic support of Ray's owners, Russ Wohlers, Earl Lasher, Elizabeth Gingrich and Jack Sikma.

Ray's Boathouse: Seafood Secrets of the Pacific Northwest is the work of exceptional people who believe in—and love—what they are doing.

Thank you, one and all.

Barry Provorse, Publisher
Petyr Beck, Editorial Director
Documentary Media LLC

INDEX

A

Alaskan weathervane scallops 166
Almond Biscuit Shortcake with Berries 145
Ancho chile 166
Ancho Chile Mayo 85
Anchovy Vinaigrette 56
Appetizers 25-47
    Coconut Prawns 31
    Dungeness Crab & Corn Fritters 29
    Grilled Salmon Skewers 30
    Manila Clams 36
    Pacific Oysters on a Spoon 36
    Pesto-Marinated Prawns 40
    Pesto-Marinated Sea Scallops 43
    Ray's Cafe Seafood Margarita 26
    Ray's Crisp Fried Calamari 44
    Ray's Pink Scallops 34
    Roasted Garlic Cheesecake 45
    Seafood Platter 46
    Shrimp Spring Rolls 38
    Shrimp-Stuffed Artichokes 41
    Smoked Salmon Cubes 33
    Smoked Scallops 37
    Thai Mussels 28
Apples
    Deep-Dish Apple Pie 142-143
Artichokes
    Preparation 121
    Roasted Tomato and Artichoke Ragoût 121
    Shrimp-Stuffed Artichokes 41
Asian Spinach Salad 53

B

Ballard, WA 20
Basil Oil 55
Belon oysters 67
Bering Sea red king crab 166
Black cod
    Applewood-Smoked Chatham Strait Black Cod 134
    Ray's Boathouse Black Cod in Sake Kasu 132
Blackening spice 166
Blood Orange Vinaigrette 60
Brownies, Double Chocolate Walnut 163
Butter, Chardonnay Prawn 119

C

Cabbage, Braised Savoy, and Serrano Prosciutto 135
Caesar Salad 52
Calamari
    Ray's Crisp Fried Calamari 44
Chambord Sabayon 140
Chanterelle mushrooms 91, 130, 166
Chard, Wilted Rainbow 119
Chateau Ste. Michelle 165
Chatham Strait black cod 166

Cheesecake
    Ray's Maple Pumpkin Cheesecake 150-151
    Roasted Garlic Cheesecake 45
    White Chocolate Cheesecake with Caramel Glaze 158-159
Chinook salmon (see King salmon)
Chittenden Locks, Hiram 9
Chocolate
    Chocolate Cake with Molten Chocolate Center 156-157
    Double Chocolate Walnut Brownies 163
    Ganache 140
    Scharffen Berger Chocolate Indulgence 140
    White Chocolate Cheesecake with Caramel Glaze 158-159
Chowder
    Ray's Clam Chowder 63
    Ray's Crab & Corn Chowder 63
Chutney
    Bing Cherry Chutney 107
    Granny Smith Apple & Dried Cranberry Chutney 112
    Spiced Peach-Currant Chutney 30
Cinnamon Roasted Squash Seeds 64
Cioppino, Ray's Northwest 77
Clams 67
    Classic Clam Linguine 73
    Manila Clams 36
    Ray's Clam Chowder 63
    Ray's Northwest Cioppino 77
    Seafood Risotto with Morels and Chanterelles 91
    Smoked Seafood Salad 59
Cod, black
    Applewood-Smoked Chatham Strait Black Cod 134
    Ray's Boathouse Black Cod in Sake Kasu 132
Cod, ling
    Steamed Alaskan Ling Cod 116
Coho salmon
    Grilled Alaskan Coho Salmon 96
    Oven-Roasted Whole Coho Salmon 112
    Teriyaki Coho Salmon 105
Columbia River sturgeon (also see Sturgeon) 115
Copper River coho (silver) 101
Copper River king salmon (also see King salmon) 49, 100-101, *101*
Copper River salmon 95
Copper River sockeye (also see Sockeye salmon) 101
Couscous, Tabbouleh 96
Crab
    Alaskan Red King Crab Legs 88
    Bering Sea Red King Crab Tempura 60
    Black Pepper Dungeness Crab 87
    Dungeness crab 26, 29, 81
        Preparing 85
    Dungeness Crab & Corn Fritters 29
    Dungeness Crab & Rock Shrimp Cakes 84
    Dungeness Crab Cakes 82
    Ray's Cafe Seafood Margarita 26

Ray's Crab & Corn Chowder 63
Ray's Northwest Cioppino 77
Seafood Platter 46
Crème Brûlée 148
Crisp, Yakima Peach & Blackberry 146
Crustaceans 80-93
Alaskan Red King Crab Legs 88
Black Pepper Dungeness Crab 87
Dungeness Crab & Rock Shrimp Cakes 84
Dungeness Crab Cakes 82
Sea Salt Spot Prawns 92
Seafood Risotto with Morels and Chanterelles 91
Curry Oil 96

D

Dabob Bay oysters 67
Dashi 166
Deep-frying 44
Desserts 138-163
Almond Biscuit Shortcake with Berries 145
Chocolate Cake with Molten Chocolate Center 156-157
Deep-Dish Apple Pie 142-143
Double Chocolate Walnut Brownies 163
Lemon Mousse 153
Lemon Mousse Torte 161-162
Mixed Nut Tart 154-155
Ray's Maple Pumpkin Cheesecake 150-151
Scharffen Berger Chocolate Ganache 140
Scharffen Berger Chocolate Indulgence 140
Vanilla Bean Crème Brûlée 148
White Chocolate Cheesecake with Caramel Glaze 158-159
Yakima Peach & Blackberry Crisp 146-147
Dungeness crab (also see Crab) 166

F

Farro 167
Farro Pilaf 127
Fennel-Horseradish Cream 37
Fettuccine with Alaskan Weathervane Sea Scallops 72
Fiddlehead ferns 111, 167
Frisée 167
Frozen-at-sea salmon 108-109

G

Garlic
Garlic-Infused Olive Oil 92
Roasted Garlic Cheesecake 45
Gingrich, Elizabeth 18, *18,* 19, 23, 153
Gore, Bruce 108-109

H

Halibut 167
Grilled Alaskan Halibut 124
Pan-Roasted Halibut Cheeks 122
Parmesan-Crusted 120
Hama Hama oysters 70
Heirloom Tomato Salad 55
Heirloom tomatoes 167
Herbed Cream Cheese 41
Honey-Ginger Vinaigrette 53
Hong, Thai *33*

Horseradish-Apple Slaw 68
Horseradish Cocktail Sauce 46

J

James Beard Foundation America's Classic Award 22

K

Kaseburg, Mauny 15
King crab 88
King salmon 95
Grilled Copper River King Salmon 99
Poached King Salmon 106

L

Lasher, Earl 18, *18,* 44
Lemon
Lemon Aïoli 44
Lemon Caper Butter 126
Lemon Mousse 153
Lemon Mousse Torte 161-162
Lentil, Black, Chanterelle Ragoût 130
Leonetti Cellars 165
Lichtenberger, Ray 14, 23
Ling cod, steamed 116
Linguine, Classic Clam 73
Loughborough Inlet 81
Ludvigsen, Wayne 15, 20

M

Madras curry powder 167
Major Grey's mango chutney 167
Mango Papaya Salsa 75
Manila Clams 36
Mignonette 168
Mirin 168
Morel mushrooms 91, 111, 168
Mushrooms
Chanterelle 91, 130, 166
Morel 91, 111, 168
Mussels 67, 78-79
Penn Cove mussels 67
Ray's Northwest Cioppino 77
Seafood Platter 46
Seafood Risotto with Morels and Chanterelles 91
Smoked Seafood Salad 59
Thai Mussels 28

N

Nova Sauce 46
Nut Tart 154-155

O

Oils
Basil 55
Curry 96
Garlic-Infused 92
Olympic Mountains *6-7, 9*
Oysters 16, 67, 70, *71*
Olympia 49, 67, 70
Pacific 67, 70
Pacific Oysters on a Spoon 36
Pan-Fried Oysters 68
Seafood Platter 46

P

Panko 168
Paprika, smoked 169
Parmesan Crisps 65
Parmigiano-Reggiano cheese 52
Pea vines 168
   Sautéed 99
Peaches
   Spiced Peach-Currant Chutney 30
   Yakima Peach & Blackberry Crisp 146-147
Penn Cove mussels (also see Mussels) 28, 67, 78-79, 168
Pie, Deep-Dish Apple 142-143
Pilaf, Farro 127
Pink scallops (also see Scallops) 168
   Ray's Pink Scallops 34
Polenta 123, 137
Potato Salad, Warm Fingerling 118
Prather, Jeff 165
Prawns *21, 24, 26, 27*
   Chardonnay Prawn Butter 119
   Coconut Prawns 31
   Pesto-Marinated Prawns 40
   Ray's Cafe Seafood Margarita 26
   Ray's Northwest Cioppino 77
   Sea Salt Spot Prawns 92
   Seafood Platter 46
   Seafood Risotto with Morels and Chanterelles 91
   Spot prawns 49

R

Ragoût
   Black Lentil Chanterelle Ragoût 130
   Roasted Tomato and Artichoke Ragoût 121
   Spring Ragoût of Morels, Ramps and
         Fiddlehead Ferns 111
Ramps 111, 169
Ramseyer, Charles 20, *20*, 21, 22, *22*, 25, 95
Raspberry Mignonette 46
Raspberry Vinaigrette 50
Ray's Boathouse *1-23*
   Cafe 10, 11
   Catering 11
   Chef's staff 22
   James Beard Foundation America's Classic Award 22
   Kids' Dock-Fishing Derby *14*
   Kitchen *5, 13*
   Lobby *17*
   View *6-7, 9, 11*
Relishes
   Sun-Dried Tomato–Kalamata Olive Relish 45
   Tomato–Kalamata Olive Relish 131
Rhubarb Compote 124
Rice Cakes, Sesame 132
Risotto, Seafood, with Morels and Chanterelles 91
Roasted Red Pepper Emulsion 97
Rockfish 115
   Spicy Blackened Red Rockfish 136
Rowley, Jon 14, 15, 16

Rub, Cumin 129

S

Sabayon, Chambord 140
Sake kasu
   Black Cod 132
   Paste 169
Salad dressings
   Anchovy Vinaigrette 56
   Basil Mayonnaise 102
   Basil Oil 55
   Blood Orange Vinaigrette 60
   Chef Ramseyer's Caesar 52
   Garlic-Infused Olive Oil 92
   Heirloom Tomato Vinaigrette 129
   Honey-Ginger Vinaigrette 53
   Raspberry Vinaigrette 50
   Smoked Seafood Salad 59
Salads
   Asian Pear-Jicama Slaw 61
   Asian Spinach Salad 53
   Bering Sea Red King Crab Tempura 60
   Boathouse Salad 50
   Chef Ramseyer's Caesar Salad 52
   Heirloom Tomato Salad 55
   Horseradish-Apple Slaw 68
   Smoked Seafood Salad 59
   Walla Walla Sweet Onion Salad 56
   Warm Fingerling Potato Salad 118
   Wasabi Slaw 102
Salmon 9, 10, 12, 14, *15*, 21, *94*, 95-113
   Fresh vs. frozen 108-109
   Grilled Alaskan Coho Salmon 96
   Grilled Copper River King Salmon 99
   Grilled Salmon Skewers 30
   Oven-Roasted Whole Coho Salmon 112
   Pan-Roasted Copper River Sockeye Salmon 110
   Poached King Salmon 106
   Ray's Cafe Salmon Burger 102
   Ray's Northwest Cioppino 77
   Seafood Risotto with Morels and Chanterelles 91
   Smoked Salmon Cubes 33
   Smoked Seafood Salad 59
   Teriyaki Coho Salmon 105
Sambal oelek 169
Samish Island, oysters *71*
Sauces
   Ancho Chile Mayo 85
   Basil Mayonnaise 102
   Chardonnay Prawn Butter 119
   Cilantro Lime Cream 137
   Creamed Sweet Corn Sauce 111
   Creole Sauce 136
   Fennel-Horseradish Cream 37
   Garlic-Ginger Black Bean Sauce 116
   Green Curry 74
   Horseradish Cocktail Sauce 46
   Lemon Aïoli 44

Mango Papaya Salsa 75
Nova Sauce 46
Orange Tarragon Butter Sauce 82
Pinot Noir Sauce 99
Raspberry Mignonette 46
Ray's Emulsified Butter 88
Roasted Red Pepper Emulsion 97
Sesame Plum Sauce 31
Sweet Chili Dipping Sauce 29
Tartar Sauce 68
Wasabi Emulsion 133
Scallops 34, 37, *42,* 43, 67, 72, 74
    Fettuccine with Alaskan Weathervane Sea Scallops 72
    Pan-Seared Alaskan Sea Scallops 74
    Pesto-Marinated Sea Scallops 43
    Ray's Pink Scallops 34
    Seafood Platter 46
    Smoked Scallops 37
    Smoked Seafood Salad 59
Scharffen Berger chocolate 139, 140, 169
Seafood Margarita, Ray's Cafe 26
Seafood Platter 46
Seattle 9, 12, 14
Sesame Plum Sauce 31
Shellfish 14, 66-79
    Classic Clam Linguine 73
    Fettuccine with Alaskan Weathervane Sea Scallops 72
    Pan-Fried Oysters 68
    Pan-Seared Alaskan Sea Scallops 74
    Ray's Northwest Cioppino 77
Shilshole Bay 14
Shortcake, Almond Biscuit, with Berries 145
Shrimp
    Dungeness Crab & Rock Shrimp Cakes 84
    Ray's Cafe Seafood Margarita 26
    Shrimp Spring Rolls 38
    Shrimp-Stuffed Artichokes 41
Shurat, Glenn 81
Sikma, Jack 18, *18,* 46
Skookum Inlet oysters 67, 70
Smoked paprika 169
Smoked Seafood Salad 59
Smoked Tomato Soup 65
Smoking process 32-33
Sockeye salmon 101
    Pan-Roasted Copper River Sockeye Salmon 110
Sole
    Pan-Seared Petrale Sole 126
    Pecan-Crusted Petrale Sole 118
Soups 62-65
    Ginger Butternut Squash Soup 64
    Ray's Clam Chowder 63
    Ray's Crab & Corn Chowder 63
    Smoked Tomato Soup 65
Spinach salad (see Asian Spinach Salad)
Spot prawns (also see Prawns) 81
    Sea Salt Spot Prawns 92

Spreads
    Herbed Cream Cheese 41
Squash Seeds, Cinnamon Roasted 64
Steaming fish 116
Strawberries, Balsamic Marinated 124
Sturgeon 115
    Cumin-Rubbed Sturgeon 129
Sun-Dried Tomato–Kalamata Olive Relish 45

T

Tabbouleh Couscous 96
Tart, Mixed Nut 154-155
Tartar Sauce 68
Tempura, Bering Sea Red King Crab 60
Thai Green Curry Paste 74
Thai Mussels 28
Tomatoes
    Heirloom Tomato Salad 55
    Heirloom Tomato Vinaigrette 129
    Roasted Tomato and Artichoke Ragoût 121
    Smoked Tomato Coulis 123
    Smoked Tomato Soup 65
    Sun-Dried Tomato–Kalamata Olive Relish 45
    Tomato–Kalamata Olive Relish 131
Torte, Lemon Mousse 161-162
Totten Inlet oysters 67, 70
Triad Fisheries 109

V

Vancouver Island 67

W

Walla Walla sweet onions 169
    Walla Walla Sweet Onion Salad 56
Walla Walla wine 165
Walleye pike 169
    Pan-Seared Columbia River Walleye Pike 131
Walnuts, Candied-Spiced 50
Wasabi 169
    Emulsion 133
    Slaw 102
Westcott oysters 70
Whidbey Island 78
White fish 114-137
    Applewood-Smoked Chatham Strait Black Cod 134
    Cumin-Rubbed Sturgeon 129
    Grilled Alaskan Halibut 124
    Pan-Roasted Halibut Cheeks 122
    Pan-Seared Columbia River Walleye Pike 131
    Pan-Seared Petrale Sole 126
    Parmesan-Crusted Halibut 120
    Pecan-Crusted Petrale Sole 118
    Ray's Boathouse Black Cod in Sake Kasu 132
    Spicy Blackened Red Rockfish 136
    Steamed Alaskan Ling Cod 116
Wine cellar 9, *164,* 165
Wine director *19,* 165
Wohlers, Russ 14, 18, *18,* 81, 92
Woodward Canyon 165